Getting
The Job
Done

BOOKS BY

Kenneth L. Adelman

◆

African Realities
(1980)

The Great Universal Embrace
(1989)

The Defense Revolution
Co-written with Norman R. Augustine
(1990)

the chief executive press

GETTING THE JOB DONE

KENNETH L. ADELMAN

whittle direct books

Photographs: Norman R. Augustine by Bret Littlehales, page 5; Katharine
Graham by Larry Fink, page 17; Tom Wolfe by Michael O'Brien, page 33;
General Charles A. Horner by Pam Francis, page 51; Justice Sandra Day
O'Connor by Larry Fink, page 63; John H. Johnson by Paul Elledge, page 75.

Library of Congress Catalog Card Number: 92-80343
Adelman, Kenneth L.
Getting the Job Done
ISBN 1-879736-06-3
ISSN 1060-8923

the chief executive press

The Chief Executive Press presents original short books by distinguished authors on subjects of special importance to the topmost executives of the world's major businesses.

The series is edited and published by Whittle Books, a business unit of Whittle Communications L.P. Books will appear several times a year, and the series will reflect a broad spectrum of responsible opinions. In each book the opinions expressed are those of the author, not the publisher or the advertiser.

I welcome your comments on this ambitious endeavor.

William S. Rukeyser
Editor in Chief

To Cal

—who gets so many jobs done,
so kindly and so successfully.

Luckily we love many, many things together,
as well as each other.

C O N T E N T S

INTRODUCTION

"W"hy an interview?" the legendary trial lawyer and sports owner Edward Bennett Williams once asked me. "Because," I responded, "cross-examination reveals much more than a monologue."

Interviews have immediacy and poignancy, as I've found while conducting nearly 50 of them for *The Washingtonian* magazine. And interviews are highly personal. Anyone interested in people is attracted to interviews. This I discovered early in adolescence from *Playboy*. While school buddies lunged for the photos and the sex-advice column, I most enjoyed those long and sometimes wacky *Playboy* interviews. (This admission undoubtedly confirms my teenage daughters' suspicion that I was a total nerd at their ages.)

Much later, in 1977, I proposed becoming a *Playboy*-like interviewer for *The Atlantic*. What could be more fun than asking famous people nosy questions? My plan for a "What I've Learned" interview feature didn't materialize then, but 10 years later, after my stint with the government, *The Washingtonian* granted my wish.

Last year, after interviewing Ben Bradlee, the now-retired executive editor of *The Washington Post*, I hatched the idea of doing a new series of interviews with chief executive officers and other extremely successful people on how they do their work. I wanted to explore the practical aspects of leadership and success. This book is the result.

Norman Augustine, the CEO of Martin Marietta, says that every winning sports team has a couple of players who take charge at the critical moment and push the team on to victory. Those players aren't necessarily hired to take command. They are not elected by the other players. They just emerge.

But is there more to it? How exactly do people at the top get their jobs done? How do leaders lead?

As the interviews progressed, insights emerged, often in the form of revealing details and examples. And certain common qualities of leadership appeared. For instance, the methods that author Tom Wolfe used to brief himself about the bond business so that he could evoke it persuasively in *The Bonfire of the Vanities* will strike a chord with any CEO who has had to master a new market or company in a hurry.

I interviewed all these people at their places of work, and the sessions were as varied as the subjects. Sandra Day O'Connor and Katharine Graham listened carefully to each of my questions, paused for thought, and answered precisely in full sentences, even in full paragraphs. Quite different was John Johnson of *Ebony* and *Jet* magazines, who could have given a sparkling interview without any interviewer. I practically had to interrupt as his stories came tumbling out. General Charles A. Horner, who ran the 1991 air war against Saddam Hussein, wore his camouflage flight suit and spoke over the roar of jets taking off outside his window at Shaw Air Force Base. Tom Wolfe and I became reacquainted over fruitcake and coffee from a silver tray in his quiet, almost Victorian New York apartment.

All six of these people know how to create opportunities that didn't exist before or to seize opportunities that others passed up. All depend heavily on skillful personal relations. While outsiders tended to focus on General Horner as a selector of targets, he considered his main job managing and encouraging people. Norman Augustine considers technical skills less important than human relations, even in his technical business. John Johnson once placed an easel beside his desk with a list of employees he couldn't afford to lose. That way, he had to think every day about how to support, motivate, and thereby keep them.

These interviews are about how people at the top make things work, especially when it comes to problem-solving. Aristotle observed that people enjoy mastering any activity, but that they most enjoy mastering the complex ones. Augustine, Graham, Wolfe, Horner, O'Connor, and Johnson have mastered some of society's most challenging activities and felt much enjoyment. They share the joy with us.

Within the pages of this unique publishing venture, we'll occasionally present some information about Cessna Aircraft Company, including our products, our corporate philosophy and some of our activities and achievements that I believe will be of interest to you.

By producing a broad line of Citation business jets, we are providing the finest and most cost-efficient transportation for more than fifteen hundred companies located throughout the world.

We are fully aware that our worldwide leadership in this industry is not based simply on building excellent aircraft, but also on our well-proven and continuing commitment to support our valued customers.

We hope that the thoughts expressed on CEO-related issues in this and future books will be interesting and beneficial to you.

I'd welcome hearing any ideas that you may have on these subjects.

Sincerely yours,

Russell W. Meyer, Jr.
Chairman and Chief Executive Officer
Cessna Aircraft Company

Cessna Aircraft Company · One Cessna Boulevard · Wichita, Kansas 67215 · 316/941-7400

Cessna
A Textron Company

Chapter One

THE LONG VIEW

F alling tides do not lower all boats. Norman R. Augustine, chairman and CEO of Martin Marietta, heads one of America's 100 largest companies and main defense contractors, with 60,500 employees. Despite the defense industry's sharp decline—U.S. defense spending has decreased nearly 25 percent in real dollars since 1985—Martin Marietta's defense business is in its 17th year of growth in sales and earnings. Defense contracting represents some 80 percent of the $6.1 billion company's operations.

Martin Marietta's debt amounts to 27 percent of its total capital. Managing nearly 1,000 contracts now, the company is approaching the largest backlog in its history, equal to about twice annual sales, and it has been winning most of the contracts it bids on—62 percent in 1991—while the industry average is 27 percent.

Augustine was born in Denver in 1935 and went east to Princeton University, where he received undergraduate and master's degrees in aeronautical engineering. He became an engineer and later an executive with Douglas Aircraft and Vought Missiles and Space.

He jumped from industry to government, serving two tours in the Pentagon and holding five positions, the last as under secretary of the Army from 1975 to 1977. Then this big man (6 feet 2 and 220 pounds) joined Martin Marietta as vice-president of Aerospace Technical Operations. He became president and chief operating officer in 1986 and, two years later, chairman and CEO.

NORMAN R. AUGUSTINE
Chairman and chief executive officer, Martin Marietta Corporation

Augustine has chaired the Advisory Committee on the Future of the U.S. Space Program and the Defense Science Board and sits on other government, corporate, and charitable boards, including the Red Cross and the Boy Scouts. He is a four-time recipient of the Defense Department's highest civilian award, the Distinguished Service Medal.

When not hard at work, Augustine is hard at play. He backpacks, reads, collects stamps, handcrafts dollhouses, plays tennis, and follows professional sports—his son-in-law, Mark Alarie, plays basketball with the Washington Bullets.

Augustine and his wife of nearly 30 years, Meg, have a son and a daughter. The family has taken many adventure vacations over the years—dog-sledding in the Arctic, climbing a volcano in the Antarctic, hot-air ballooning in Africa, rafting through the Grand Canyon, snorkeling in the South Pacific, driving covered wagons along the Oregon Trail, and photographing polar bears in the Northwest Territory. Augustine has also managed to write two books: the lighthearted management tutorial *Augustine's Laws* and a heavier geopolitical tome, *The Defense Revolution*, which I co-wrote.

Sitting in his Bethesda, Maryland, corporate headquarters, we discussed getting the job done.

◆

Q. *While the defense sector is sinking, your defense business is swimming along nicely. How come?*

A. Because years ago we foresaw what's happening now and prepared for it. It's known as swimming along underwater. In 1985 our 10-year forecast predicted a substantial downturn in defense beginning in 1986. We arranged ourselves accordingly.

Q. *Hold on a minute. How—during the depths of the Cold War, when President Reagan wasn't even talking to Soviet leader Yuri Andropov—did you envision less defense spending?*

A. We looked beyond our company and industry. Some warning signs were obvious: Reagan would be leaving office after 1988, having completed a defense buildup beyond what any successor would do. We watched the federal budget deficit grow and realized the nation was on a financial collision course. We also thought there were clear signs that the Soviet economy could not indefinitely support defense spending at such a high level.

If the U.S. deficit was out of control and something had to be done, that "something" meant defense cuts. Since most discretionary federal funds go for defense, some cuts in the federal budget meant big cuts in the defense budget and even bigger cuts in its procurement budget. This is the part of the budget that keeps the defense industry afloat.

In addition, we saw the Pentagon positioning companies to take enormous risks. It took real discipline in the '80s to avoid "winning" contracts that would end up costing the company plenty in the '90s.

The winners then look like losers now. Over the past few years, defense contractors have lost nearly $8 billion on tenuous fixed-price development contracts. They shouldn't have taken them on. We didn't.

Q. *Were you unique in the business to foresee such a decline?*

A. We were perhaps unique to start preparing in 1986 for the downturn by raising our research-and-development spending, bidding on more contracts that build up a backlog, cutting costs, and refusing to underprice many huge fixed-price development contracts.

Wisest of all, we didn't play in the acquisition frenzy of the mid-'80s.

Since defense contractors were riding high, everybody wanted to own a defense company—even other defense companies.

A defense company then cost up to twice its annual sales. Today it's one-half of sales and sinking. That's a decline by a factor of four in less than five years. We preserved cash, which is why our leverage is around 25 percent today, whereas the industry average is 40 percent.

Q. *How did you make the right strategic appraisal when others did not? How did you avoid the "group think" of those days?*

A. We avoided "cocooning," or drawing into ourselves. Many executives listen primarily to those in their own community. I've gone out of my way to listen to academics, environmentalists, politicians, even defense critics, who say things we don't necessarily like to hear. Many defense contractors weren't looking at the larger picture because they were so busy filling orders.

Q. *Other executives think listening to geopolitics or grand economics or environmentalists is a waste of time. But you found that to be your salvation.*

A. In engineering terms, people often miss the signals buried in the noise. They dismiss what they don't like to hear. The practice of shooting the messenger tends to dry up the supply of messengers.

Q. *Tell me about obstacles you faced when implementing this strategic decision. Some people must have urged you to take orders, at whatever price.*

A. It took courage by our whole team to stick to our course. In the '80s we lost a number of competitions. Other companies bid far below us on big fixed-price contracts. They bid aggressively and hoped their lawyers would later find a way out if their engineers couldn't.

We spent many weekends back then trying to figure out what was wrong with us. Why can these others do things for so much less than we can? The answer, we now know, is that they couldn't. That's why some are now striving to stay solvent.

We also resisted the buying frenzy—when management adrenaline outweighed management judgment. Executives can become macho about buying companies. They begin to chase this rabbit. Even though it starts to look like a mouse, they keep chasing it as if it were a gazelle.

We exercised discipline, fixed the top price we'd pay, and decided when to fold. So we folded most times. Today this seems wise, since most of those companies weren't worth what people paid for them.

It also took courage to prepare for a rough '90s by hiking R&D spending in the '80s. We were initially so excited about that decision that our president went to New York in 1984 to tell analysts and investors about it. They listened for a bit and literally ran out of the room to sell our stock, causing it to drop 11.5 percent in five days and continue to fall for two years. We wondered what went wrong. Apparently they hoped we were about to be the victim of a hostile takeover, to be broken up and sold off to the Japanese at a big, fast profit to shareholders. "Why boost research, which won't pay off for 10 to 15 years?" they asked. That's a waste of resources, they figured, since the average shareholder stays with the company for less than two years. To their credit, the people who then ran this company took the hit. Our stock dropped, but we went roaring ahead on research. Today that looks like a great decision.

Q. *Why? What research paid off?*

A. We've made a unique kind of seeker guidance system for missiles, systems that see at night, computers and systems that can detect targets with no humans involved. One day this effort should help enable a machine to read handwritten addresses on envelopes to sort the mail.

Q. *But if such research doesn't pan out, you're out the money.*

A. True, research involves risk. But we believed our research would ultimately produce important products. And it did. A similar investment a decade earlier led to the laser system that guided the first missiles fired in the 1991 Gulf War. This helped hold U.S. casualties to such low levels. Yet the investment community was too impatient at the time to wait for those products to appear.

Q. *Why is that a better approach than just selling what's needed now?*

A. You can't live on only short-term investments if you're a high-tech company, as we are. The half-life of most technologies today is between two and 10 years. Products we sell 10 years out will be altogether different from those we sell today. In the year 2000 we won't be able to give away the products we're making now.

Q. *American business is criticized for living from quarter to quarter, if not month to month. That's not true in your case.*

A. Our executives had the courage of their convictions and the good fortune of being relatively safe in their jobs. Their board of directors wasn't demanding next-quarter results. Not all managements enjoy that situation.

Q. *You mention having a cooperative board. Does that mean a rubber-stamp board?*

A. No. That's costly. When you really need advice—and being CEO is a lonely job—it's nice to be able to turn to somebody informed but independent enough to be objective.

Some CEOs seek board members like they seek employees. They don't want talented people around who could be a threat. I feel just the opposite: it's hard to look bad when you're surrounded by talent.

Q. *How do you recruit good people for your board or in your company? What do you look for?*

A. First off, personal attributes. Is the person decent, of high integrity? Without that, there's no sense going any further. Second is job qualification—basic talent and knowledge—which is usually the easiest part to find. Third is motivation. You want somebody willing to go the extra mile. Motivation will beat mere talent nearly every time. Finally, teamwork. I've had bosses who sought to create conflict among subordinates in order to sharpen issues. That's not me. I believe in encouraging people to speak out, but in a spirit of teamwork.

Q. *Do you call references?*

A. Absolutely. Past performance is by far the best indicator of future performance. We depend, as a criterion for advancement, upon whether someone has left "monuments," or significant accomplishments, along the way. If there have been no past monuments, there probably won't be any future ones.

Q. *By rewarding monuments, aren't you encouraging people to grab the headlines?*

A. No, because we emphasize teamwork and react badly when someone grabs headlines. I've watched many people fail in their careers by fixating on how they appeared to others. It's like a football player running downfield to catch a pass and then looking up in the grandstand to see if everyone is watching. Sooner or later the football will hit him on the head. The best way to get ahead is to do your current job well and not worry about the future. The future tends to take care of itself.

Q. *How do you overcome obstacles?*

A. First, recognize there is an obstacle. Trying to run through walls is not a great way to build a career. Second, have a plan. Third, execute the plan. And fourth, change it if it doesn't work. Don't just keep plowing into the wall, but look for a door. Fortunately, most walls have doors or at least windows in them.

Q. *Don't you get discouraged along the way?*

A. Sure, but remember that what seems discouraging today may not even be remembered in a month or year. I think about how I enjoy solving problems. I try to welcome them. After all, solving problems is what my job is all about—ranking right after *avoiding* problems.

Developing the Patriot missile, for instance, was one problem after another. The project began in the mid-1960s and was nearly canceled at least twice by the Pentagon and even more times by the Congress. The media blasted it, as did most everyone during its development phase, which took 18 years. Critics asked why we needed it, said it wouldn't work, wondered about the price, and so on.

As it turned out, the Patriot did a fine job of intercepting Scud missiles. Raytheon, the prime contractor, and ourselves launched a crash effort to build enough missiles to engage Scuds over Israel and Saudi Arabia. Some missiles came off our Florida assembly line and engaged a Scud over Israel two days later. Real just-in-time manufacturing!

Q. *Tell us your big mistakes.*

A. The first missile I ever had any particular responsibility for blew up—due to a problem I believe I might have caught. And I believed strongly in the Cheyenne, the Army's attack helicopter of the 1960s, which was eventually canceled for being too complicated and costly.

But my all-time career mistake was to support the acquisition of a midsize company with good management, which had 91 percent of the market in a burgeoning new field. Its customers, large corporations, thought it was a wonderful company. So we bought a major stake—and within six months the company was drowning in red ink.

Q. *What went wrong?*

A. The company had too rosy a forecast, and we believed it. Since the company wished to retain its near monopoly market share, it kept investing in new factories and other assets before the orders came in. The executives overestimated demand, and the whole shebang went tumbling, fast and hard. Leverage works in both directions.

From that I learned a big lesson. While it's good to have enthusiasm, you also need people on the sidelines being coldly objective. They check human enthusiasm against harsh reality. We all tried to be objective but were too close to the purchase.

Q. *What's your comparative advantage as CEO?*

A. The ability to judge people—whether they're honest, motivated, and team players, and whether they know what they're talking about.

Q. *So it's your people skills rather than your slide-rule skills?*

A. Yes. Early in a career, slide-rule skills are more important. If all the missiles you build blow up or the electronics make smoke, you'll never get to manage anybody. But people who fail in high positions fail for personality reasons, not for lack of skill. Anyone who's made it up three or four layers into management knows the job. Then personality and human skills become more important.

Most CEOs move through 10 layers of management in their career. At lower levels, some can manage by intimidation. Being a threatening taskmaster works when you've got a dozen or so people working for you in the same room. But when you have 50,000 to 100,000 people working for you around the world, most of whom will never even see you, it's hard to manage by intimidation. You don't scare anybody when you're that far away. Then you have to manage through leadership.

Q. *In your business, do you need a lot of creativity?*

A. That's true throughout the high-tech arena. If you're not creative, you'll soon be history.

For instance, microchips, now used in everything from automobiles to thermostats, change from one generation to the next in about two and a half years. If you let your creativity slide for five years, you'll be two whole generations behind. Then you couldn't give your product away, let alone sell it.

Q. *So how do you engender creativity?*

A. Allow people to fail. You can't encourage creativity and not tolerate failure. You have to give them idea space. And you have to develop rewards for being creative. Look at baseball. The difference between a .300 hitter and a .250 hitter is about one hit a week. A .300 hitter is a star, and a .250 hitter is a journeyman player.

Thus in research the difference between being very successful and failing may be one hit a year, or even one a career. Two of my friends invented the semiconductor integrated circuit. So profound was the impact that in Japan it's called "industrial rice." They did other important things in their lives, but that hit changed the course of humanity. They didn't need to do more to be enormously successful.

Alexander Fleming discovered penicillin by noticing that a culture he was growing did not survive in some mold that had accidentally contaminated his specimen. He had the innovative spirit to perceive the implications of this, whereas most of us would have washed the slide and started over. There are many such examples.

Management must push and recognize creativity. When I worked in the Pentagon, I wondered whether I would have paid attention to a fellow who showed up wearing a stocking cap, speaking broken English, and saying he had an idea for a device to end World War II. Maybe I wouldn't have recognized an Einstein.

Q. *How do you make an environment for creativity?*

A. We expect everybody to be creative. There is push by the R&D and technology people, who come up with new products that might well be useful, and pull by a customer wanting something. Studies show that, of all new products introduced, those thought up by the senior management have by far the highest failure rate. Next are those conceived by middle management. The most successes come from the lower levels, especially from people in the field talking to customers.

Q. *But they need support to get a new product through the system.*

A. That's true. Creative people disrupt the status quo. That's inconvenient to some managers. If business is good—you're making the world's best propellers and somebody wanders in with an idea for a jet engine that doesn't even have a propeller—management is inclined to kick him or her out. Leaders must be willing to upset the status quo.

Q. *Tell us about leaders. From your experience in business and government, what are common traits among leaders?*

A. I've had many great bosses. I tell any young person coming up, "If you don't have a great boss, go get one. Your career will be in grave trouble if you don't." Leaders are people of high integrity. When they say something, you can believe them. You can't be a leader if people don't believe you. Leaders work awfully hard. They know what they're doing, are able to make decisions, and have the courage of their convictions.

They go out of their way to give feedback to subordinates. If something isn't going well, they say so and recommend something different. If things are going well, they share or even deflect the credit to others. In a word, leaders find talented people, set goals, and mostly get out of the way. Above all, successful leaders lead by example.

Q. *What personality works the best for a leader?*

A. The kind you'd choose in a friend. Managers get things done right, and leaders get the right things done. The distinction is important.

Leaders are individuals with few big holes in their abilities. Studies show that your ability to advance depends on the strength of your weakest attribute. Leaders have relatively strong weak points. In general, it's not possible to make up for weak points by strength in areas where one excels.

Q. *Are you optimistic about leadership and business in America?*

A. Yes. But to compete successfully, we will need more managers who understand how people unlike themselves think, people who can understand and gain respect from those of different backgrounds.

That's needed not only to expand into global markets but also to deal successfully in a more diverse America. By the year 2000, some 85 percent of those entering the U.S. work force will be other than native-born male Caucasians. So it will take a broader, more tolerant, perceptive individual to be an effective leader.

Q. *How does a company build a successful corporate culture?*

A. A relatively small group sets the standard and shows the way. It's just like on a good athletic team; a couple of people become the acknowledged leaders. The coach doesn't appoint them. They aren't elected. But they're the ones, when it gets tough, who step out front. Everybody watches them and figures, "That must be the way you do it around here."

Q. *Why do people fret about the future of U.S. business?*

A. Because they realize that many of our obstacles are self-created. Some have been caused by greed. Some executives, particularly in the '80s, tried to make the fast buck without adding value or producing anything. This is a hollow strategy. Financial engineering simply won't work over the long haul. You don't add anything to a business or country by cutting the pieces of a business apart and gluing them together in a different pattern. Instead you've got to have something new come out the factory door—new ideas and new products.

In the 1980s, while many American businesses were busy pursuing financial engineering, the Japanese were busy running their factories. Now we're paying the price for that.

Q. *You're known for having 15-minute meetings.*

A. I startle people in the Pentagon when I ask to see a senior official for 15 minutes. The staff is initially suspicious, thinking I'm trying to get a foot in the door, but they've discovered that I mean it. After 15 minutes, I get up and walk out. To schedule 15-minute meetings keeps things moving along.

Q. *Do you have other unusual management techniques?*

A. Well, I do my paperwork at home or on airplanes. I do almost no paperwork in the office.

Q. *You don't read during the day?*

A. No, I spend my day in meetings or on the telephone. I devote the day to customers and employees. I communicate a lot by notes, which is a double-edged sword. It's very impersonal—frankly, I never liked getting notes from my bosses—but it's efficient. It saves time, I can do it at night, and it puts something on the record. The recipient keeps the paper around until the task is done.

I have two fabulous secretaries, one for scheduling, phone calls, and general office management, and the other for dictation, mail, and special projects. When I'm traveling I receive a Federal Express package each day and send one back the next day. So I'm seldom more than a day or so behind on my mail, even on the road.

Q. *Why do you insist on having a round conference table?*

A. That puts everybody on an equal footing. I dislike sitting at the head of a table; it inhibits ideas. In the normal conference room, the person at the other end of the table may have the best idea but is so far away that it's tough to convey it. A round table makes everybody an equal part of the conversation.

Q. *That fits the trend towards more consensual management.*

A. It does. No one person has all the answers. In fact, a CEO knows less about any given part of a major decision than others in the room. Your lawyer has legal information you don't have; your engineer gives technical advice beyond your knowledge; your accountant knows the figures and financial reports; the personnel representative has spent years as a labor negotiator; and so on. They're giving you conflicting advice, and you have to sort it out. You have the ultimate responsibility.

Q. *How do you know who's right?*

A. Know the track records. Who built the monuments?

Q. *Chance is a big factor in life, isn't it?*

A. It surely is. I didn't become a forest ranger because a teacher sent me off to a college where they didn't teach forestry. I met someone on a train who steered me into aeronautical engineering. I'm with Martin Marietta because I went to a huge luncheon one day and happened to sit next to someone who told me about the company. I'm married to a wonderful woman that I met by chance who was born in Sweden, halfway around the world from me.

Had all that not happened, I might have become a forest ranger. Today, I'd be sitting on a rock in Yosemite instead of here in my office—and I would probably be the happiest guy in the world.

SENSIBLE BUSINESS DECISIONS GOT YOU WHERE YOU ARE. THIS ONE TAKES YOU WHERE YOU WANT TO GO.

You've led your company through times in which others have failed.
Thanks in no small part to your ability to act quickly and decisively.

But as the pace of the world quickens, you wonder if your company
can continue to lead if it must follow airline schedules. For more than
1,500 businesses worldwide, the answer is no. They fly Citations.

It may surprise you to learn that a number of these companies are
really not all that big. Yet.

THE SENSIBLE CITATIONS

Cessna
A Textron Company

Chapter Two

Taking Chances

K atharine Graham achieved greatness by having the Washington Post Company thrust upon her. "Watch my little Kate. She'll surprise you," said her father, the financier Eugene Meyer, who bought the *Post* in a 1933 bankruptcy auction. But no one expected that she would do so with her father's own newspaper business. Not even Meyer, who left the paper instead to Graham's husband, Philip. He served as president of the company until his suicide, caused by manic-depression, in 1963.

Though painfully shy, Kay Graham walked into the *Post* days after her husband's death to announce that she would keep the paper. In fact, she'd even help run it, though, as she recalls now, "I didn't even know how to give directions to a secretary."

Born in June 1917 in New York City, Graham graduated from the University of Chicago in 1938 and began work as an entry-level reporter with the *San Francisco News*. For the next six years she worked off and on for the *Post* editorial and circulation departments as "the low person on the totem pole."

When she decided to step in, the *Post* was still locked in a circulation war with the *Washington Star*, which finally folded in 1981. The *Post* now has a 51 percent market penetration on weekdays and a whopping 68 percent on Sundays. In addition to the *Post* and *Newsweek*, the company owns four television stations and 52 cable systems, as well as a newspaper in Everett, Washington; Kaplan Educational Center, which

KATHARINE GRAHAM
Chairman, Washington Post Company

prepares students for educational tests; newsprint operations; and one-half of the *International Herald Tribune*.

"It's one hell of a story, because she really did walk in there without formal business training and with a temperament that did not make things easy," says Graham's friend and mentor Warren Buffett, whose Berkshire Hathaway Inc. owns around 15 percent of the Post Company's stock. "She had the will to succeed and she did. It's like a stutterer overcoming the handicap and becoming a great public speaker."

Graham succeeded by choosing a strong staff and making courageous decisions. Her defining moment came in 1971, when she decided to publish the Pentagon Papers. "The decision was hers alone," said Ben Bradlee, whom she had previously chosen as managing editor and who was then urging publication. "It was the most important editorial decision of the last 25 years."

Graham remains chairman of the board. Her son Donald Graham, who has been publisher of the *Post* since 1979, was promoted to president and CEO of the company in May 1991.

In her eighth-floor office in the *Post* building, with black-and-white photos of her father and husband displayed behind her desk, we discussed getting the job done.

◆

Q. *You were tossed into running the operation without much training, weren't you?*

A. Without *any* training. I was totally unprepared. Because of the death of my husband and our owning controlling shares of the Post Company, I had several choices: try to learn about the company, let someone else run it, or sell it. I set out to learn what went on here.

Q. *But during the period right after your husband's death, how could you decide to run this huge organization?*

A. The *Post* wanted me to—at least the people that mattered did—and I wanted to do it. But I didn't view my being here as really running the company. I merely figured that as long as I held controlling shares, I should know what was going on.

Q. *So initially you didn't intend to run it?*

A. No. Fritz Beebe, the CEO, would do that. I expected to be passive, at least while I learned.

Q. *At what moment did you realize, "God, I have responsibility for this place"?*

A. Only later—and gradually. What I first assumed to be true was not in fact true, namely that things would stand still, that the people who had been running things would go on running them, without much involvement with me. But problems instantly arose, and things needed to be decided. I soon saw that things needed to be done that weren't getting done. That's when I stepped in. My first big decision was moving Ben Bradlee in as assistant managing editor.

Q. *When you first took over, did you have clear goals? Did you think, "Well, there are three things I'd like to do here"?*

A. No. I figured everything was all right, and it would just keep on being all right. People included me in meetings, told me about some things going on, and complained to me about things not going on. But I didn't feel qualified to make big decisions.

Q. *Until hiring Bradlee . . .*

A. Even that decision was gradual. People started running up to me saying that the place needed more talent and energy. Then two or three people applied for the job of assistant managing editor, which brought the issue of changing the way things were being done to a head.

Q. *How do you go about hiring people? What do you look for?*

A. Others to help make big decisions with me. I've learned never to make a big decision by myself. Hiring is the hardest though the most critical thing an executive does. It's usually best to promote from within. While there are times when you simply have to go out, that's dangerous . . .

Q. *Because outsiders don't know the company culture?*

A. And you don't know them. It's hard to completely check on someone who's been working elsewhere. Most people want to be nice; they won't tell you the whole truth. The only way to get at that, I've discovered, is to go and see the reference in person. Someone's much more apt to tell you the truth in person than on the phone.

Even if you find that someone is bright, it's hard to tell whether he or she will fit into the organization, is administratively able, and fair and decent.

The most common mistake is in "Peter Principling." Somebody may be quite good at a certain level and not at a higher level. A skilled salesman or writer may not be a good administrator. A good reporter may not make a good editor. The jobs sound similar, but they're really very different.

Q. *The higher up you go, the more important people skills become?*

A. Absolutely. The minute you manage anybody, people skills become critical.

Q. *What motivates people?*

A. Liking their job and their workplace. Financial rewards. Those who perform with excellence should receive some stock or cash rewards. This ought to be administered with great thought and not just handed out.

And people must have leeway. Doing what the boss wants may not be doing the best thing. If you hire good people, you won't agree with all their decisions, but you have to back them up. It's critical for the staff to feel that you're behind them—that if they make a mistake, you're going to understand, and they'll be free to correct it.

Q. *Yet you haven't been shy about changing people.*

A. If they don't live up to what the company needs, if they disagree on goals and methods, then you just have to move them out.

Q. *Do you talk to new executives about the goals?*

A. Sure. They must know what you expect. You must know what they expect.

Q. *I ask because Ben Bradlee has said that he went day to day without any real plan in mind. His only goal was to put out a better newspaper tomorrow than he put out today.*

A. Ben wasn't running a business. He was running an editorial product.

When Ben came, we couldn't have said that the *Post* should be thus and thus in 10 years. Editorial products are not too easy to plan. You know a paper's weaknesses and try to address them. Above all, you have to listen to what people are saying and change with the times. You especially have to learn what young people brought up on television want.

Q. *Your business is unique, since the business side is quantifiable while the product side is not.*

A. But you have a quantifiable measure of approval in circulation.

Q. *Yes, though the* National Enquirer *has a great circulation, but no one would equate that product with excellence.*

A. So you look and listen. Read the paper and compare it to the competition. And listen for whether others say you're producing a good product. An editor has to be extremely sensitive and intuitive—to operate by the seat of his pants.

The *Post* is unique as both a mass and a class paper. Most people think of it as a national and international paper, but we have always wanted a mass readership. That's unlike other papers. *The New York Times* is just class—they have a large readership in a relatively small percentage of their market, as does the *Los Angeles Times*.

Q. *What does the* Post *do differently to succeed in both mass and class?*

A. Have enough to interest people who aren't in the State Department. That means offering comics, features, sports, style, lots of city and suburban news, and obituaries—the bread and butter stuff.

Q. *I always thought that writing obituaries was the ultimate revenge—to have the final word on people.*

A. Actually, obituaries are among the most important parts of any paper, because they're read and because people care very, very much about what they say. *The New York Times* has elevated obituaries to an art form, especially for prominent people. We have much improved ours.

Q. *British papers are incredible on obituaries, which are by far the most amusing part of their papers.*

A. And in a community like Washington, nothing is more personal.

Q. *A few moments ago you emphasized the importance of consulting others. Yet there are defining moments when you're on your own. For you that happened when deciding on whether to publish the Pentagon Papers in June 1971, after the Nixon administration won a court injunction stopping* The New York Times *from continuing to publish them.*

A. That situation was peculiar. The *Times* had been enjoined the previous day. They had received the Papers three months before and had been summarizing the material. Management had a big discussion with their lawyers over whether to print them, and I think, in fact, one of their law firms resigned or was fired over that issue.

By the time the *Post* received the material, I simply assumed we were going to print it. My coexecutive Fritz Beebe, also a lawyer, had come down from New York for someone's farewell party. He knew that we had received the Papers and that there was controversy about publishing them. He went over to Bradlee's house and walked in on a heated argument; our lawyers were saying that we just couldn't publish the material.

Ben and the other editors wanted to print it. I attended the going-away party. In fact, I was on my lawn making a toast to the departing business manager when they called me. We had missed the deadline for the first edition, which went out with a lesser story on the front page and several promotion pages in the space reserved for the Pentagon Papers. The editors got me on the telephone and pressed me to decide. I had only a few minutes, since the paper's second edition was set to go.

Q. *Had you been privy to these arguments before the call?*

A. No.

Q. *So they hit you blind?*

A. Yes.

Q. *That's not a very good management technique, is it?*

A. Well, no, but this was a crisis. Those things happen. It wasn't planned that way.

The lawyers' objections had been heard. Fritz recommended, as he told me on the phone, that we wait. We had announced a few days before that our stock was going public. So at that exact moment, we were halfway public—having announced it but not having sold the stock yet. The company was as vulnerable as it could be.

I heard our business people worry about the dangers, our lawyers talk about the risks, and our editors talk about the opportunities. Each got on the phone with me one by one, and each felt so strongly. Their arguments were good. The editors said that everyone knew we had these Papers, and it was essential to publish them if we were going to be a first-rate paper. I said, "Well, I guess we ought to go."

Q. *So how did you decide?*

A. How? Well, I don't know. I didn't think it through. There are moments when you have to intuit, and I did then. Some people enjoy conflict and dust-ups. I wish I did, but I don't. I felt somehow that we couldn't function as a newspaper if we let this pass. Fritz helped in a funny way: I heard a tone in his voice which said that on balance he wouldn't publish the Papers, but he obviously didn't feel publishing would be an utter disaster.

Q. *But you must have realized your serious obligations on the business side, going public with the stock, the potential suits, the television and radio licenses jeopardized . . .*

A. Not if you have two minutes to decide, you just can't think about all that. Then, it's your antennae telling you that publishing seems like the right thing to do.

Q. *How much of business is intuition and how much is practicing sound management techniques?*

A. There's not a sharp distinction. Intuition has to be based on a solid knowledge of people and substance. You can't intuit well without a solid base.

Q. *But for that decision you lacked a solid base but obviously made the right judgment.*

A. That may be because I had no time to ponder. Often I think people spend too long making a decision. Warren Buffett—in many ways the most brilliant person I know—decides things very fast because he has such a vast body of information.

Q. *But you fret over decisions.*

A. I sure do, though I don't recommend it for others.

Q. *Then why do you do it?*

A. Because that's my nature. I'm a worrier, a constant worrier. I fret. I chew on myself. If I make a mistake, I live with it too long. So I do all the things I'm not supposed to do.

Q. *You've said that if you had to write one book, it would be a book on management.*

A. I have come to believe that getting and maintaining good management is as interesting and difficult a problem as any. I find it so fascinating in a bizarre way, since I came cold to it.

I used to look at other companies and think, "Boy, there's a well-managed company. I'd like ours to be like that. I wonder what they do to make it work so well." Then, five years later, I'd read that the company fell on its face. I used to think every company ran better than ours, which caused considerable pain to the managers here.

Q. *Tell us the concluding chapter of the management book you may never write.*

A. It would contain simple lessons: Know your business. Decide which issues really matter and work on those. Have good people around you. Delegate authority.

Q. *Let's take a concrete issue—*Newsweek. *What really matters in that business now?*

A. That conditions have changed considerably and that newsweeklies are threatened more than ever by the surfeit of other magazines and so many more news outlets—television news, cable, CNN, C-Span.

Newsweeklies used to be the authoritative collector of the week's news. That clearly isn't the case anymore. However, *Newsweek* still has

EARLY IN HIS CAREER,
MR. PALMER TURNED IN HIS CONVENTIONAL DRIVER
FOR SOMETHING WITH CONSIDERABLY MORE LOFT.

Years ago, Arnold Palmer quit using automobiles for traveling to golf tournaments. For almost as long as we have built Citation business jets, Arnold Palmer has flown them.

Without the speed, convenience and reliability of Citations, Arnie says he couldn't possibly compete on the tour, design more than 100 golf courses, and manage his far-ranging business activities.

Mr. Palmer's game is golf, but his business is winning. So is his business jet.

THE SENSIBLE CITATIONS

Cessna
A Textron Company

a circulation of 3.3 million in the U.S. and 22 million readers. That's a whole lot of readers.

You have to change with the times, but you can't jolt your readers by suddenly changing to a whole new concept. At *Newsweek* we have to think hard about what people still want to know at the end of a week and deliver that to them in a thoughtful, interesting package.

Q. *You talk about not jolting your readers, but that's what the* Post *did in its biggest innovation under your leadership when it suddenly replaced the "Women's Pages" with the "Style" section.*

A. I wish there had been a better way. We really did jolt our readers.

Q. *What's wrong with that?*

A. Well, it's all right if you're absolutely sure the venture will be successful. But we jolted readers unnecessarily hard. We abandoned features we didn't need to abandon—like those on fashion, celebrity houses, and food. People want to read about those things. In Washington they want to know who attends a White House dinner. People look for that in a newspaper. We dropped those things for a while, which was silly.

Q. *Speaking of parties, I have to ask about yours. You entertain loads of people at your home in Georgetown. How can you see somebody socially and have your newspaper criticize him or her publicly? How do you balance those two?*

A. I don't balance them. The two are totally separate. Government officials and journalists in Washington need a lot of discourse. It's important for people coming into government to get to know us and for us to get to know them. From that professional traffic comes friendships. Some people think there's something wrong with this, but I don't. I think it's healthy. When a government official knows me and the editors, he's able to call and register his complaint or correction.

Q. *But how? Once a story is written, it's out there. It's hard to retract. I know you have those little correction boxes, but they don't do much good.*

A. Correcting this way is important. It's essential not to repeat a mistake or get it into the system and then have it constantly regurgitated. And it's critical for an editor and/or reporter to know someone had it wrong.

Q. *But you must have had difficulties when you've been friendly with Billy and all of a sudden, bam, there's a harsh article about Billy in your paper. What do you say to him?*

A. If I think the harsh article was justified, I say nothing.

Q. *But Billy is probably going to say something to you. Most Billys do, don't they?*

A. Yes, most do. If the article was justified, I'll mumble something to Billy. If Billy is justified, I'll say something to the editor responsible.

But I'll never go out and say that I disagreed with what the paper did. It was ultimately my responsibility. And when I register my feelings with the editor, he or she may not agree with me. That happens when you give your people autonomy.

Q. *Does it cause you pain?*

A. Yeah, it can. If we've been unfair to somebody or made a big mistake, it causes me pain. It doesn't happen very often, though.

Q. *Any mistakes you care to talk about?*

A. No.

Q. *But it's an interesting position you're in, since your friends see your product every day.*

A. And they feel it personally. They presume I've approved everything that's in the paper, which of course I haven't. Outsiders may see me as having written a story or caused it to be written. It's wrong to think that I run downstairs and tell someone to write this or print that.

Q. *Why? Won't they take your recommendations?*

A. Yes, they will—if I have a good case. Otherwise . . .

Q. *When reporters are working on some big story, do you ever stop them?*

A. Occasionally I'll say, "Gee, do we have to do that?" Or, "Why are we doing that?" Usually they have a good reason.

Q. *Do you ever spike a story?*

A. No. I never have. There was a claim recently that I killed a story about Senator Charles Robb. [Virginia beauty queen] Tai Collins said this on the *Larry King Live* show. This woman claimed that Mrs. Lady Bird Johnson called me and I intervened. It was just nuts. I called up Larry King and told him it wasn't true. Besides, I've never killed a story—never, in my whole 28 years at the *Post*.

Q. *Why not? Wouldn't that be part of your job?*

A. First, I'm usually not aware of stories beforehand. Secondly, I really wouldn't kill a story. I might tell an editor that I think the story is a mistake or to think about it. But I've never killed one. One time Henry Kissinger called and asked me to kill a story about him that Maxine Cheshire was finishing.

Q. *About his personal life?*

A. Yes. I really did beg the editors downstairs not to publish it, but of course they did—and with added enthusiasm. The next morning brought an enormous explosion from the other end of the telephone. It took a while, but eventually Henry and I got together again.

Q. *Did you explain to Dr. Kissinger that you tried to stop the story?*

A. He was so mad, he was screaming so loudly at me, that he couldn't have heard.

Q. *But that's a case of playing on a friendship with you in order to stop a bad story, right?*

A. No. Henry knew which editors were in charge of what. He'd complain to the appropriate editor about a story he didn't like, unless the article was written by [reporters] Maxine Cheshire or Sally Quinn. Then he'd call me and scream, assuming somehow that as a woman I had more control over them than their editor.

Q. *Do you get involved with individual stories?*

A. Very rarely. I get involved in deciding whether, and how, a section needs improvement, but not in individual stories.

Q. *What did you have to learn first when you took over?*

A. Everything—company values, what makes a business good or bad, how a manager works. Simple things, like what our profit margins should be. I didn't know anything, so it's impossible to describe what was most lacking. If I had known what it was going to be like, I might have chosen another course.

Q. *But you had worked on the* Post *for years and at the* San Francisco News *before that.*

A. I'd reported at the *News* and worked on lowly editorial things here.

Q. *So you knew something about a newspaper.*

A. Something, but more importantly, I cared. Warren Buffett thinks that the main thing going for me was that I really loved the paper. I cared deeply about it and the magazine. I wouldn't have gone to work at all if this had been a furniture business. I had been so tightly involved with my father and my husband that I had to make the *Post* survive. I had a stake in seeing their hard work succeed.

Q. *It was competing head-to-head with the Star?*

A. No, it wasn't competing. That was the problem. The *Post* was fifth in a field of five city papers. It was sold to my father in bankruptcy with a circulation of about 51,000. He really started with it at the bottom.

Q. *Do you worry about the future of your business, since young people don't read as much and everyone relies more on television for their news?*

A. We own cable and television stations . . .

Q. *But your base is print.*

A. Yes. I believe so much in print that it's up to us to devise ways to assure its survival.

Q. *Like what?*

A. Like making sure it will appeal to those who have first seen the news on television—with graphics, some short and snappy stories, and interpretative articles to explain what all this news means. Viewers can never understand complicated subjects from the one-minute spot on television. Democracy depends on that understanding, so democracy depends upon print.

Q. *You already talked about hiring people. How about firing people? How do you do that?*

A. There's no good way. But when it has to be done, you have to do it. I tell the person as much as I can without hurting his or her feelings unnecessarily. The person is bound to think you're being unfair and usually says so.

But it's very trying, because other people never seem to see themselves realistically. If I were failing in a job, I'd realize that, but most people seem not to. That's very strange.

It's also amazing to look up the personnel file of someone about to be fired. You find so many great appraisals right up to the bitter end.

Q. *Reviewers are chicken.*

A. Yes, managers are reluctant to tell people they aren't doing well and why. They should help the person work on shortcomings, but that rarely happens.

Q. *Watergate must have been a lonely time for you. The* Post *was pursuing a story of wrongdoing by the president of the United States. It seems like such a great story, but few other papers were pursuing it with you. What made you persist?*

A. That, again, was a question of backing. Ben Bradlee had been here seven years by then, and we'd worked together intimately. I trusted him, the editors under him, and the reporters under them. And I didn't much trust the Nixon White House.

Q. *Was it putting pressure on you?*

A. Four organizations challenged our FCC licenses for two Florida TV stations, which sent our stock way down. Every license holder had to renew every three years then.

Q. *And that's usually an automatic extension?*

A. Usually, but not in this case. The challenging groups contended that we weren't doing a good job.

Q. *And that scared you. Did you think the challenges were politically motivated?*

A. Of course it was political. We heard Nixon's tapes later when he said that our stations were coming up for FCC renewal and that something should be done about this.

Q. *You had faith in Bradlee. But did you ever think that pursuing the Watergate story might not be worth the risk?*

A. No. My philosophy has been to strive for the best editorial product, though doing so may cost us some advertising cancellations. Well, that story could have cost us the whole company, had we been wrong.

Q. *Didn't that cause you to sweat?*

A. It certainly did. I tried to figure out if we could survive the rest of the Nixon administration—for four years, then three years, then two years. It was just awful until the first break came—nearly a year after we got on the Watergate case—when James McCord admitted that funds from the Committee to Reelect the President had been used to buy the silence of the Watergate conspirators.

Q. *So it worked out.*

A. Yes. But even if I had decided that chasing Watergate could cost us the company, there was no way I could go downstairs and say, "Let's stop." All of us thought the reporting was accurate.

Q. *Yet there must be some instances where business interests figure into editorial decisions.*

A. Oh, there's some gnashing of teeth, both at *Newsweek* and the *Post*, when we have to report some health matter that may cost us millions of advertising dollars.

Q. *How so?*

A. Cigarette advertising is at risk when we run stories about the dangers of smoking, and automobile ads sometimes suffer when we write about auto-safety problems.

Q. *Do you think newspapers are biased? For instance, would the* Post *have gone after your friend John F. Kennedy, as you went after Nixon, had you known then of Kennedy's personal habits?*

A. I think we would have. Whether we would have pursued his involvement with girls, I'm not sure. It's a different era now about that kind of thing. Besides, I think the girls were pretty harmless until Judith Exner came along. I think we would have reported that.

Q. *Because of her connection with the Mafia?*

A. Yes. If somebody just has girls, that doesn't interest me much.

Q. *Don't you think it's an indication of faulty character?*

A. Sometimes, but everybody is fallible. The Gary Hart episode was a matter of character, since it was so indiscriminate. Do you want a president like that? I don't.

Q. *So you had no qualms about having a* Post *reporter follow Hart?*

A. A *Post* reporter didn't follow him. I don't like spying on people, but when someone invites it, that's different. And when a presidential candidate disappears every night, that tells you something. It's too much.

Q. *So character is important in this business.*

A. Yes. But whether the president has one girl or two girls . . .

Q. *Do you have a manual of how many girls you'd allow?*

A. No manual, but I would draw the line where the behavior affects his credibility and job. Clearly, Gary Hart's did. Clearly, I don't think Kennedy's did, even in retrospect, except for Judith Exner.

Q. *Does it make you think less of Kennedy?*

A. Yeah, it does. I knew there were girls around, but I certainly had no notion of the extent of his problem.

Q. *Do you think the press has become too personal?*

A. It isn't only the press but also the government that requires excessive statements about finances and behavior. Appointments to the Supreme Court are a good example. It has become best for any president who wishes to avoid big confirmation difficulties to appoint a nonentity. Even then he can get into trouble.

Q. *Let's go back to how you get the job done. Did you face a lot of difficulties as a woman running a huge organization?*

A. Initially I didn't realize how much women were discriminated against. It wasn't until I started to run things that I realized the barriers. After all, I had grown up in an atmosphere that taught women to go along with things, that men were smarter, that we couldn't be as able as they were. It took the women's movement to make me understand all this.

Q. *Why did you continue to think that way when you were the boss—and a good one?*

A. I was so dense that I didn't see when I was being condescended to. For instance, I went to dinner parties for years where women and men separated after the meal.

Q. *The men would go into the heavy talk and the women would discuss their makeup?*

A. Yes. Eventually it dawned on me that I spent all day on editorial and business issues and didn't need to leave the serious talk after dinner. That hit me like a firecracker one night at [the columnist] Joe Alsop's house. I said that if he wanted to separate us, I'd go home, which was fine with me, since I had enough work to do there.

Joe got terribly upset and said I just couldn't do this to him. They would talk for just a little bit. I said, "No, Joe, this will go on for an hour, and that's an hour I can use." Joe stopped and others followed. My behavior, I'm happy to say, helped break this habit in Washington.

Q. *Did you worry that you weren't being nice to the ladies, since you indicated you didn't want to be with them?*

A. No, I didn't think of that. [*Laughter*]

Q. *But initially, when coming to the* Post, *you felt inadequate as a woman.*

A. That's because I *was* inadequate, as a professional. Being a woman complicated these feelings.

Q. *Was there a moment in your career when you thought, "Hey, I'm not inadequate anymore. In fact, I've done a hell of a job!"?*

A. No. I have to tell you, there never was. I can't say that.

Q. *But you should. You should say to yourself, after all these years, that you've done a hell of a job.*

A. All right, I'll try.

THE VERY FIRST CITATION PRODUCT
TO GO UP IN THE AIR WASN'T A BUSINESS JET.

Future Home Of
cessna/citation
SERVICE CENTER
Opening Fall 1971

Before the first Citation ever rolled off the line, we built the first service center dedicated exclusively to maintaining the aircraft.

Now, nearly 2,000 Citations later, there are Citation Service Centers located 45 minutes apart throughout the contiguous United States, and Authorized Citation Service Stations around the world.

When you own a Citation, we're here to take care of the aircraft so the aircraft and you can do what you do best. Take care of business.

THE SENSIBLE CITATIONS

Cessna
A Textron Company

Chapter Three

THE RIGHT STORY

H e's a singular sensation. Americans devoured *The Bonfire of the Vanities* and were uplifted by *The Right Stuff*. Yet Tom Wolfe stands apart from New York literary circles. That's both his choice and theirs.

Born in Richmond, Virginia, on March 2, 1930, to an agronomist father and artistic mother, Wolfe has stood out ever since. He graduated with honors from nearby Washington and Lee University in 1951 and tried his arm at professional baseball. The New York Giants turned him down.

So Wolfe went to Yale instead of to the pitcher's mound. His doctorate in American studies came in 1957, after a dissertation that focused on communist attempts to organize American writers in the 1930s and showed, he summarized later, "how easy it is to organize writers because they're so deracinated, feel such need for community, and have so few organizations to join."

As a beginning reporter, Wolfe himself had few organizations to join. He applied to 53 newspapers and took the only resulting job offer—with *The Springfield Union* in Massachusetts. He stayed for two and a half years. Later, while covering local and Latin American news for *The Washington Post*, he received a Washington Newspaper Guild award for his reports on Castro's new Cuba. In 1962 he joined the *New York Herald Tribune*, where a strike led him to try a pop-culture piece for *Esquire*.

After struggling through an agonizing encounter with writer's block,

TOM WOLFE
Author

Wolfe was on his way. He was in his element in pop culture and in the new journalism—using fictional devices for nonfiction reporting.

Cranking out some 40 impressionistic reporting pieces over the next two years, Wolfe became the talk of the town. According to columnist Liz Smith, "Wolfe caused severe jealousy and outrage pangs throughout the U.S. literary establishment when he sprang right out of pop culture's forehead to become a star practically overnight."

Adding his insult to their jealousy, Wolfe assailed the pretensions and hypocrisies of the "culturati." He even went after that holy of holies, *The New Yorker*, whose bland style he panned in a series of 1965 articles entitled "Tiny Mummies! The True Story of the Ruler of 43rd Street's Land of the Walking Dead!" Writers got mad, and *The New Yorker* got even: for the next two decades the magazine reviewed none of Wolfe's books. Then it reviewed *The Bonfire of the Vanities*—and panned it.

Millions of Americans came to know and adore Wolfe through *The Right Stuff*, his acclaimed literary account of America's brave, aw-shucks astronauts. Meanwhile, his colorful turns of phrase, like "radical chic," "the Me Decade," and "the right stuff," became everyday expressions.

Then, like an explosion, *The Bonfire of the Vanities* erupted in 1987. It had all the Wolfian hallmarks—jillions of exclamation points, baroque language, and words that were a joy to read. The novel also established Wolfe's credentials as an expert outside observer of the 1980s financial scene, even though he knew little about it before starting the book. The methods he uses, and engagingly describes, to master unfamiliar information apply far beyond the literary world.

Since his marriage at age 47 to Sheila Berger, a former art director at *Harper's* magazine, Wolfe has tried to keep his home life similar to the one he had growing up: private and uncomplicated. His parents never showed anxiety about life. "To this day," he says, "I can't stand to see parents wrestling over the macaroni of their lives in front of a child." Wolfe and Berger have two children, Alexandra, 11, and Tommy, 6. The only pastime he admits to is window-shopping.

It was an experience entering Wolfe's New York apartment and having him graciously take my wraps. We sat in his study, which was adorned with elaborate Victorian drapery. The bright sunlight blocked everything but his round head. With his hair parted down the middle and his high collar, he looked like a member of Calvin Coolidge's cabinet as he explained how he gets his job done.

◆

Q. *You've written about Las Vegas, stock-car racing, architecture, computer whizzes, Black Panthers, Mercury astronauts, a go-go dancer, New York City—and everything else under the sun. How do you choose topics?*

A. From the first my instincts were journalistic. I looked for subjects that hadn't been written about, such as the rock 'n' roll composer and producer Phil Spector, "the first tycoon of teen," as I claimed he was. He was the first teenager to make a million dollars in a business aimed strictly at other teenagers.

I did a series of articles for the short-lived *World Journal Tribune* in 1966 about the novelist Ken Kesey and his commune, a group known as the Merry Pranksters. The year before, I had published my first book, *The Kandy-Kolored Tangerine-Flake Streamline Baby,* and I was looking for a subject for a second one. Somehow Henry Robbins, my editor at Farrar, Straus & Giroux, had come across some Xeroxed copies of letters Kesey had sent to Larry McMurtry from Mexico, where Kesey was in hiding from California authorities on drug charges after jumping bail.

All I saw in it at first was a magazine piece, a story about a *real* fugitive. There were three popular fictional dramas about fugitives on television at that time, one of them called *The Fugitive*. When I finally caught up with Kesey and the Merry Pranksters, I began to realize I was onto something more interesting than mere life on the run. Kesey and his Pranksters were, in fact, a primary religious group, very similar in spirit, motivation, and evangelical practices to the early Zoroastrians, early Hindus, and early Christians.

I think it can be argued that the influence of people like Kesey and his East Coast counterpart, Timothy Leary, did more to change this country in the 1960s and 1970s than the war in Vietnam. In any event, as soon as I could, I expanded my newspaper series on the real-life fugitive into the book *The Electric Kool-Aid Acid Test*, about the psychedelic religious movement.

As you can see, the word *journalism* is not one that I shrink from. Quite the contrary. What journalism refers to is writing today about what is happening today. I find that irresistible. Even *The Right Stuff* started off journalistically, as a series of articles for *Rolling Stone* magazine at the time of NASA's final mission to the moon, Apollo 17.

Q. *How important is the selection of a topic for you? Or can you write about anything?*

A. In a big effort, like a book, the topic has to engage my curiosity. It has to arouse a passion that goes beyond any possible end result. The worst way to choose a topic is simply in order to make money.

Around 1972 Henry Robbins and I had lunch to talk over what I should do next. It was time to begin another book. I had three ideas—American high schools, new American religions, and the astronauts. The one least interesting to a publisher, he said, was the astronauts. But I became overwhelmingly curious about them.

Q. *Why?*

A. Because I had an obvious question which hadn't been answered: What makes somebody willing to sit on top of a 36-story rocket and wait for somebody to light the fuse? What on earth prepares someone to do that? Makes someone even want to do that? It was so far from anything I could imagine doing!

I had read some about the astronauts—that they were all first or only sons, that four of the first seven had "Jr." after their names. I could identify; I was a first and only son and had "Jr." after my name. They were from small towns—which I wasn't—they were all Protestants and believed to be from very stable families. That turned out not to be true—Scott Carpenter's family had broken up early in his life, but this was hidden at the time. They all supposedly had very stable marriages. Yet one of the wives had been divorced and had remarried, and one of the astronauts had separated from his wife, but this was also papered over.

Anyway, I wondered, "Is this what does it—what makes them sit on that 36-story rocket and wait for somebody to light the fuse?"

It turned out that these personal, ethnic, and religious factors had little to do with it. They merely reflected the general profile of the military officer corps in the 1950s. None of these factors was unusual for that crowd. Learning this led me into something far more interesting—the code of the "right stuff" among flyers.

Sheer curiosity also led me to turn the Ken Kesey story into a book. I discovered that Kesey's movement was like a primitive religion. Most early religions used drugs or extreme physical states such as fasting, sensory deprivation, or wild dancing to alter bodily metabolism and achieve ecstatic states. Wine, still part of the Christian Communion service, was apparently used as a psychedelic. This was absolutely fascinating to me. Such primary religious movements pop up continually. Some change the world. Most don't.

The case with *Bonfire* was a bit different. Deciding to write that book meant writing fiction after a career of nonfiction.

Q. *At 50, trying something new.*

A. Past 50, when I started on it.

Q. *Why break a successful pattern?*

A. For two reasons, one personal. I'd wanted to be a writer since I was 5 or 6, when my father was editing a farm journal, the *Southern Planter*. In his mind, he was an agricultural scientist. But in my mind, he was a writer. So I wanted to be a writer.

Q. *That's the "Jr." part of you.*

A. Yes. And in college you learn that to be a serious writer you have to be a novelist. That's probably still the idea.

Anyway, I started newspaper work as a way to keep body and soul together while I prepared to write novels. But then I became fascinated with what became known as the new journalism, creating a literary non-fiction. Soon I was hooked on that.

Q. *Wasn't Truman Capote's* In Cold Blood *the landmark work of that genre?*

A. It was, but the new journalism had started earlier. The writer I was watching most closely was Gay Talese. The movement was so exciting! In a literary and journalistic sense, it was new. The cutting edge. At first I wanted to see what I could do in this form, so I had little interest in writing fiction.

After I finally finished *The Right Stuff* [published in 1979], I said to myself, "Now wait a minute. I don't want to look back upon my career and say, 'Gee, what would have happened if I'd ever done a novel?'"

That was the implied rebuke to those of us who were involved in this new journalism—that we were ducking the big one. So on the

IMAGINE A CITATION
THAT'S BEEN FLYING NONSTOP
SINCE THE YEAR 1307.

That's how much flight time Citation business jets have logged.
The fleet has accumulated an incredible six million hours of service.

It's the equivalent of one Citation flying night and day for 685 years.

It took more than just one to chalk up six million hours, of course.
Nearly 2,000 Citations are now in service – the world's largest fleet.

So if you're looking for the business jet that more businesses fly, just
look up. Chances are, there's a Citation passing overhead right now.

THE SENSIBLE CITATIONS

Cessna
A Textron Company

personal side, this was a challenge I figured I ought to accept.

Q. *Another plateau.*

A. Not so much a plateau up above as another range to ride. The other side of it, my second reason, was more of a professional consideration. Back in 1973 I had written a long essay discussing the novel's decline. I predicted that if the novel had any future, novelists would have to revive naturalism. So I wanted to write a realistic novel to prove that professional point.

In 1969 I had gotten the idea of writing a big work about New York, just as William Thackeray wrote *Vanity Fair*, a big work about London—but I'd do it in nonfiction while he did it in fiction.

In fact, that's why I went to Leonard Bernstein's party for the Black Panthers, to get material. I figured it might make a chapter of such a book. But it was such a fantastic set piece that I couldn't resist writing it to stand alone.

Q. *Was there something disloyal about your going to his house and then panning it afterwards?*

A. No, I don't think so. I wasn't even invited. I went as a member of the press. One day I happened to see an invitation to the party while I was in David Halberstam's office at *Harper's* magazine. I was wandering around, killing time, waiting for my appointment, and I spotted this invitation with a phone number on it for responding.

I had passed up a similar party, to which I had been invited, for Cesar Chavez's grape workers, out at a grand mansion on the beach in Southampton. What people told me about that party was fascinating. Here were socialites in Gucci shoes and Pucci clings listening to a grape worker say, "Close your eyes and imagine that you're working in the dusty fields of the Napa Valley. You're up at 5:00 a.m. You're looking forward to a breakfast of a hot dog and Coca-Cola," and so on.

So the folks did just that, they closed their eyes and imagined themselves into the grape fields, keeping one hand on their heads because the winds from the ocean were playing havoc with their $45 hairdos, the men's as well as the women's. Fashionable men had big hairdos in those days.

I kicked myself for missing that one. So when I spotted the invitation to the party for the Panthers, I knew I just had to go. I called up the number on the invitation and accepted. I gave my name and said I was from *New York* magazine, for which I was doing a lot of work at that time.

Most likely I reached somebody working for a committee who had a yellow legal pad and was jotting down the names of people who accepted, because when I arrived at the party at the Bernsteins' apartment at Park Avenue and 79th Street, there was a little security desk in the entryway with a guest list, and my name was on it. So I went in and wandered around with a notebook and ball-point pen. I introduced myself to Leonard Bernstein and his wife, who probably assumed that anybody there to write about the event would be sympathetic to the cause. Someone was there from *The New York Times* and someone else from *The Village Voice*; they were also taking notes.

Q. *So they didn't mind people writing about it?*

A. Oh no. In fact, a photographer from *New York* magazine had Leonard Bernstein, his wife, and Donald Cox, field marshal of the Black Panthers, pose for a picture. It was one of those formal portraits, such as Farah Diba and the Shah of Iran used to pose for.

After that people figured I made it my business to write about parties. This meant that half the people wouldn't invite me over, and the other half were people I didn't know who hoped I'd come and write about them and their parties.

Q. *Whose parties you wouldn't want to go to anyway.*

A. Just for the record, I never have written about anybody's party I've attended unless I was there expressly and openly as a member of the press. In any case, I wrote about the Bernsteins' party not as part of any nonfiction *Vanity Fair* but in a long article for *New York* entitled "Radical Chic." It later became the lead portion of the book *Radical Chic and Mau-Mauing the Flak Catchers*. This was in 1970. When I finally returned to my *Vanity Fair* notion in 1981, I was very much in a mood to do it as fiction, but a particular kind of highly realistic fiction.

I had come upon the title *The Bonfire of the Vanities* in 1971 on an American Express bus tour of Florence, Italy. When we reached the Piazza della Signoria, our guide mentioned Savonarola's "Bonfires of the Vanities." The people of Florence were encouraged, and later forced, to bring out their vanities—wigs, clothes with golden threads, books by Bocaccio, false eyelashes, nonreligious portraits—and put them in a great pile and burn them. The term had a literal meaning. People actually burned their vanities in what they called "bonfires of the vanities."

Q. *To get rid of their excesses.*

A. Yes. That was the mood of those times. It's the mood in the U.S. now, though I don't expect to see any bonfires. Get rid of the fleshpots! Become ascetic! Melt down the golden calf! No, don't melt it down—you can still use it then—throw away the golden calf!

I loved the phrase so much that I instantly decided to write a book with that name someday. I had a title but didn't know yet what the book would be about. In 1981 I decided it would be the title of my long-fantasized book about New York. I also decided to turn my usual approach upside down. I had tried to write *The Right Stuff*, *The Electric Kool-Aid Acid Test*, and *Radical Chic* using the structural techniques of the novel or short story. But *The Bonfire of the Vanities* would be fiction using the reportorial techniques of journalism.

Q. *A lot of novelists try to expose themselves, mentally and psychologically. You expose other people or New York City. Why don't you reveal yourself?*

A. I suppose I'd have to psychoanalyze myself to answer that. Forty years ago it was axiomatic that the only valid literary material was the material of your own life. But that certainly wouldn't have made sense to Dickens, Balzac, or Tolstoy.

Ralph Waldo Emerson said that everyone has a great autobiography to write, if that person truly understands what's unique about his own life. But most people censor the unique parts. They think they're so strange that they won't interest anybody else.

Emerson didn't say that everyone has *two* great autobiographies to write. He said one. Many novelists have a problem: they milk their lives for one excellent book, and then they're suddenly out of material.

We live in such a wild time that I find it endlessly fascinating to write about things I know nothing about. I knew nothing about the psychedelic or hippie world. I knew absolutely nothing about airplanes, much less astronauts. When I began *The Bonfire of the Vanities*, I knew nothing about Wall Street, other than where it was physically, or the South Bronx, or the court system there.

It's marvelous, living in a country like this, in an age like ours, in which people's lives can change so rapidly. It's fascinating to learn about these things and try to bring them alive on the page. I find that much more challenging than finding the bottom line on the moral balance sheet.

Q. *Let's talk about your reporting—your trademark. Physically, how do you learn about Wall Street or the South Bronx? How do you get that job done?*

A. Reporting consists of going up to total strangers and asking them questions, the answer to which you have no right. This is not a genteel occupation. You're a beggar. It's humiliating.

There have been many great English essayists but few great English writers doing nonfiction that's based on reporting. Maybe a proper Englishman isn't going to like it precisely because it's humiliating.

In reporting, no matter what you write about, you usually have to start with one person. It's no use approaching a group and announcing, "Okay, I'm here." If you get along with one person, that person will introduce you to others. I first approached Wall Street in 1984, when things were going absolutely beautifully there. I had heard these wild stories of what was happening at the big investment banking houses.

So I called up a fellow on Wall Street who had gone to the same high school I had gone to in Richmond, Virginia. He invited me to lunch with several of his Wall Street friends. Not to overdramatize the matter, but this was a fateful lunch for me in writing *The Bonfire of the Vanities*.

Q. *What fascinated you was the jillions of dollars they managed?*

A. Not just that. It was their description of the mood on Wall Street in the mid-1980s, the psychology of the boom, the euphoria. It was their insights into the feeling of omnipotence that the boom was producing that gave me the idea for my "masters of the universe." I wanted to see this species up close.

So I asked my friend if I could go down to his office and watch what goes on. He had told me about the fervor, the warriorlike atmosphere when big bond auctions take place. I had always thought of bonds as the dullest subject on earth. Economics was dull enough, but bonds were the dullest part of economics. For years Wall Streeters specializing in bonds had been known as "the bond bores."

By the mid-1980s this had all changed. Bonds were now the big league. Stock traders were looked upon as pitiable wimps. Probably seven times more money changed hands in bonds than in stocks. For one thing, much of our national debt—of how many trillions?—is in bonds. The bond-trading floors were the gladiatorial arenas.

Anyway, my friend, who was from Lazard Frères, said, "Look, you can come down here, but we're a relatively small operation. You really should go to Salomon Brothers. That's bond central." He called up some people he knew at Salomon Brothers, who said, "Sure, come on down." They were great, gave me the run of the place.

At that time, in the spring of '84, I was ready to start writing *The Bonfire of the Vanities* for *Rolling Stone* serially, a new chapter every two weeks. It was to run for a year. I had done a 200-page outline and had it all planned out. The main character was a writer, Sherman McCoy.

When I went down to Salomon Brothers, it was spellbinding, seeing these young men—the old-timers were 41 and 42—on the bond desk with this exuberant warrior mentality. Dealing in bonds was suddenly very exciting and volatile. I felt that I should change my main character, around whom I'd written the whole outline, from a writer to a Wall Streeter.

But I'd only been to this one place, Salomon Brothers, and still didn't know much about bonds. Time was running out. I had to get the first three chapters ready for *Rolling Stone*. Anyone who looks back at the *Rolling Stone* version will see that Sherman McCoy has no occupation in those chapters. I was still debating with myself about whether to make him a bond trader.

Then I got cold feet and stuck with my outline, and Sherman McCoy was a writer. By chapter six, I must confess, I was bored with him. I never have found writers particularly interesting as people, and my own main character was becoming tedious to me. I knew I would have to revise heavily for the book version.

Writing a novel the way I did for *Rolling Stone*, doing a new chapter every two weeks, really amounts to doing a very public first draft. But

I will be eternally grateful to *Rolling Stone* and especially its maestro, Jann Wenner. If I hadn't written the book that way, I probably never would have done it at all. I had already spent nine months catatonically sitting at my desk trying to get this damned thing started!

Anyway, I rewrote the book with Sherman McCoy as a Wall Street figure, a bond salesman. It was a critical change. Back then, all this was news. When did people first start reading about the warrior life on Wall Street in the 1980s? Not until the Ivan Boesky scandal. These people were making tons of money, and the outside world had no conception of either the scale of it or the hog-stomping Dionysian spirit. One investment banker complained to me that he would go to a dinner party and sit next to a pretty girl who would ask him what he did. "I'm a bond salesman." She'd yawn and turn to the man on her other side. He said, "What am I supposed to do? Wear a sign around my neck saying FINANCIAL GIANT?"

Q. *When you go to their offices, do you question them or watch them?*

A. I don't ask a lot of questions unless that's all I can do. I'd much rather watch and ask questions later.

Q. *Are people generous in that way?*

A. Extremely. My only contribution to psychology is the notion of "information compulsion." People enjoy telling you what you don't know. That's true with me; if somebody stops me on the street to ask directions, I'm delighted, if I know the answer. If I don't, I'm resentful he stopped me. I'm gaining a fraction of a status point by knowing something he doesn't know.

So I have information compulsion too. Here I am, talking to you! Everybody likes to have someone listen to his life story. It constantly amazes pollsters and sociologists what people will tell them.

Q. *I can understand the Wall Street part, but tell us about the South Bronx part, when you wrote* Bonfire. *That seems a tougher nut to crack.*

A. I started off in the courthouse.

Q. *You just walked in?*

A. Yes, but I knew the chief administrative judge of the criminal division, who opened some doors for me. Once I was there, I met lots of different people. Court reporters—who are the stenographers who record testimony—are gold mines of information. They sit all day listening to this stuff like flies on the wall. People think they're attached to a machine, that they don't have their own ears. But they are generally well-educated, quick-minded people who know everything in the courthouse. They are repositories of the most bizarre stories. The press barely covers the courts at all. Even in big cases you won't find a reporter present except at the beginning and the end. If you sit in on a case all day, every day, as I often did, and you're not a lawyer or a relative of the defendant, people wonder why in the hell you're there.

IN 1995,
PEOPLE AROUND THE WORLD
WILL BEGIN DOING THE SIX-SECOND MILE.

You're looking at the fastest business jet in the world. At Mach .9, it does a mile in 6.06 seconds. And sprints LA-to-New York in under four hours.

It's the new Citation X. And it's the latest example of Cessna's commitment to the development of new technology. Our total investment in business aircraft research and support is now more than a billion dollars.

You can see for yourself the remarkable result of that investment when Citation X deliveries begin in 1995. But you'd better look fast.

THE SENSIBLE CITATIONS

Cessna
A Textron Company

So they come over to talk to you. I met many people this way.

Q. *Weren't you scared to walk around there?*

A. The courthouse? No. The area around it? There are areas I wouldn't walk in cold, but you can go anywhere in the South Bronx if you're with somebody who's known. I walked around in a double-breasted suit and necktie. I went into burned-out neighborhoods, illegal social clubs, housing projects, and I never tried to dress down. What good would it have done, anyway? The key is to arrive with someone who is accepted in that particular milieu. An off-duty policeman took me at night on the entire route Sherman McCoy took on his drive through the Bronx.

Q. *What do you see that we mortals don't see?*

A. Thanks for the deific compliment, but the answer is, "Nothing." If I don't make a conscious effort to turn on the radar and concentrate, I'm not going to see any more than any other mortal, I'm sure. Once I do, however, I'm on the alert for status factors—anything that shows how people rank one another or position themselves with respect to others, any particular airs they put on, or refuse to put on. These things interest me most.

I think matters of status are the key matters in any situation. *The Right Stuff* is really not about the astronauts, per se. It's a book about the competitive pyramid of flying, which is largely invisible to those outside.

Q. *Test pilots are on top.*

A. In peacetime but not in wartime. Then, fighter pilots are at the top. Test pilots who've never flown in combat feel there's a big ticket they haven't punched.

Q. *We think of American society as egalitarian, in contrast to, say, Japanese society, whose language has nine or so levels for addressing anybody from a trash man to the emperor. But you think America is very status-minded?*

A. Every country, every people, is. There are innumerable groups of statuspheres in America, status worlds in which people judge other people by the standards of competitive pyramids.

But ours is not a class-driven society in any European or Asian sense. We don't even have an upper class as such. It's our saving grace that people with money are afraid to act upper class. They bend over backwards not to.

Q. *Why is the subject of status so important to you?*

A. I think it's the key to human behavior. The concept was developed by the sociologist Max Weber, who'd roll his eyes back if he heard how it's used today to mean social climbing. He meant by it a situation, a position. Most people spend their lives not trying to rise but just to hold on to their position. That's hard enough.

Out of the slums today comes the term "dissing" people, meaning disrespecting people. That's so interesting. People will kill for dissing, not showing respect, which is a matter of status. The Civil War began—yes, because of slavery and the collision of economic systems—but really because the South felt so thoroughly dissed by the North. Crucial matters of status are often totally divorced from economic motivation.

Chuck Yeager didn't fly the X-1 to make money, or even to make colonel. He flew it because the challenge of flying at the speed of sound was at the apex of his particular statusphere, as a test pilot.

So status is absolutely fundamental. What makes someone angriest is humiliation, which creates the urge to kill at all levels of society. Humiliation is a matter of status.

Q. *I read that you had writer's block in '62 when starting with* Esquire *and again 20 years later when starting on* Bonfire. *What happened?*

A. I think writer's block comes chiefly from fear.

Q. *Fear of failure?*

A. Yes. Fear of not being able to do what you've announced you're going to do, either to yourself or to somebody else. It can also come from realizing that what you started out to do isn't worth doing. In graduate school I started a long paper on how the electric refrigerator was introduced into American life. It was very complicated. After a bit I said, "Who cares?"

Q. *How do you overcome your fear of failure?*

A. I think about Edward G. Robinson, who identified the secret of his early success as his addiction to Havana cigars. They were so expensive that he had to keep hustling to pay for them. To be young and have no money, that'll do it.

Guilt can do it too. Early on I went out to Los Angeles and spent loads of *Esquire*'s money at the Beverly Wilshire hotel while gathering material for an article about customized cars. But I couldn't write the piece. I had never written a magazine article, and that assumed enormous proportions in my mind. I don't really know why.

Q. *So what did you do?*

A. Finally, Byron Dobell, who is a great editor, just said to me, "Look, we've spent a lot of money on pictures for this supposed story of yours, about $10,000, and we've got to have a story. If you can't write it, just type up your notes. We'll get a competent writer to do the piece."

With a heavy, guilt-ridden heart, I typed up my notes, starting at eight o'clock one night in the *Herald Tribune* office after work. I started typing as fast as I could, to get it over with. Pretty soon, I realized that I'd started writing the story. The 48-page memo I wrote to Byron Dobell that night was what *Esquire* ran.

Again with *The Bonfire of the Vanities* I was doing something I'd never done before, writing a novel. I had to get it written not only for professional reasons but for financial reasons. So I put myself under deadline pressure for the serial publication in *Rolling Stone*. In this case the pressure overrode the block. I wonder if I would have ever written that novel otherwise.

Q. *Your profession is tougher than most, since your feedback is so delayed and can be so faint. You're writing* The Right Stuff *or* Bonfire *and months go by without your getting any feedback. In the corporate world or entertainment world, people come in every day and give feedback. Isn't that tough for you?*

A. It can be very frightening in many ways. Financially, for a start. Wise parents tell children never to touch their financial principal, their savings. But that's the only way I've been able to live. I never meant to spend six years writing *The Bonfire of the Vanities*, but I did. Not only did I invade principal, I massacred it. I borrowed money to an extent that shocks me even now.

After extending myself for so long, I felt suddenly, "This is air business. I'm writing all these words on a page. Can I seriously expect anybody to take these as something substantial?" My mind started playing tricks in the middle of this long journey. Because I really don't know how it's going to turn out. It's such a big gamble!

Q. *What sustains you through the desert?*

A. The subject. If I wasn't really interested, it would be awful. At the end, you're waiting for applause.

Q. *But it's a long wait.*

A. It shouldn't take so long. And meanwhile I lose the ability to be critical of the big picture. I can tell whether a chapter works, and especially whether a paragraph works, but not whether the whole structure works. I'm going through that with what I'm working on now.

I'll show parts to my wife, who is wonderful at editing since she doesn't send me valentines. She'll tell me the truth. Professional editors are apt to be a bit more wary of discouraging you.

Q. *Do you use a computer?*

A. No, I still use a manual typewriter. I can't stand anything that hums at me. It's sitting there, saying, "Okay, big boy. Let's produce!" So I use either a manual typewriter or write by hand.

Q. *You have to be tough psychologically to do this, but you've been tough in other ways too—taking on icons like* The New Yorker *early in your career. You were castigated and then ostracized for it. Wasn't that painful?*

A. It was for a week or so. When I wrote that piece in April 1965, I thought I was being rather amusing by doing a profile of the editor of *The New Yorker*, William Shawn, just the way *The New Yorker* had had so much fun doing profiles—they invented the form—of other people. So many important and famous figures denounced me when the piece came out—J. D. Salinger, who had never before, or since, uttered a word to the press; E. B. White; Richard Rovere; Murray Kempton; two columnists in my own newspaper, Joseph Alsop and Walter Lippmann.

I thought the end had come, the sky was falling in. I was relatively unknown then, a mere reporter who had never published a book.

About 10 days passed and nothing really happened—except that loads of people I didn't know sent me invitations. That was my first big lesson in the perversity of our times—unless you're accused of a felony, notoriety doesn't hurt at all. It showed me I could run into heavy literary fire and live to tell about it.

By coincidence, my first book was coming out two months later, and this controversy focused enormous attention on it. Some people were so conspiracy-minded as to think I dreamed up the affair to publicize my first book.

Actually, I never could see why people shouldn't write about the worlds of journalism and literature in the same way that journalists and writers write about people in the worlds outside. But I never got any thanks for being so eminently fair-minded.

Q. *What does it take to get the job done in writing?*

A. The most undervalued element is organization. I'm a great believer in outlining. For *The Right Stuff* I did a schoolboy outline of more than 300 pages—with a big Roman numeral I, and then a capital A, and then an Arabic 1, and so on. That's critical, I think, since what you're really doing is creating the structure.

Second, reporting is essential for any kind of writing. Reporting feeds the imagination. Balzac was always leaving his desk in the middle of a novel to see what a proper country wedding looked like or to be briefed on military financial scams. Some writers' imaginations are underfed, because they don't venture outside their own lives.

You also need keen curiosity about the subject, an intrinsic interest in finding out, which goes beyond the rewards of the writing. And you need some confidence. I think of the travails of male opera singers. They start training in their teens and turn 32 or 33 before they know whether they'll have a chance to make it. The top of that pyramid is tiny, and below the top are nothing but disillusioned nonentities. How you come by such confidence, I have no idea.

Q. *Don't you miss people?*

A. What do you mean?

Q. *Yours is a solitary work, unlike 90 percent of other occupations.*

A. I don't miss people during the day, while I'm working. I start work early, now that I have children. They get up early, so I get up early.

Before, mine was a lonelier life. I'd start work in the afternoon and work every day until midnight, taking as little time out for dinner as I could. Life's better now.

THE DAY A BUSINESS JET TAUGHT
THE SHISHMAREF FIRST-GRADE CLASS.

The Citation V's unique ability to fly long distances yet land on short airstrips has allowed it to get into some pretty remote places. One such place was the tiny, isolated town of Shishmaref, near the Arctic Circle.

When the Citation landed on a narrow snowplowed strip, children came running from the nearby school. They'd never seen a jet before.

And chances are, they may never see any others besides Citations. Unless Shishmaref builds a runway long enough for less versatile business jets to use.

THE SENSIBLE CITATIONS

Cessna
A Textron Company

Chapter Four

COMMAND DECISIONS

I n combat, a military officer's success is measured simply: did his efforts help win the war for his country or not? Lieutenant General Charles A. Horner ran the stunningly effective air war against Iraq during Operation Desert Storm. His success triumphantly validated lessons of modern warfare he had bitterly learned in Vietnam: get the job done smartly, quickly, and with a minimum loss of life. In the 1991 Gulf War's first 14 hours, his men flew more than 1,000 sorties with only one of their own planes downed. Another 111,000 sorties followed. Horner commanded more than 55,000 U.S. troops and 1,800 U.S. aircraft and supervised the entire coalition effort totaling more than 2,400 planes. They averaged 2,600 sorties each day of the six-week war. The impact of the air war on Iraq was devastating, making the 100-hour ground war a cleanup operation.

Such mastery does not spring up overnight. Known in the Air Force as a "fast burner"—someone who gets promoted more quickly than his peers—Horner has logged more than 5,200 flying hours, including 111 combat missions over North Vietnam in the mid-1960s. He had been stationed in the U.S., England, and Thailand before March 1987, when he became commander of the U.S. Central Command and Ninth Air Force, which are headquartered at Shaw Air Force Base outside Columbia, South Carolina. His forces had operated in the Persian Gulf for nearly four years before the outbreak of war in January 1991, and

LIEUTENANT GENERAL CHARLES A. HORNER
Commander of the coalition air forces, Operation Desert Storm

Horner had shuttled back and forth between that area and headquarters. In the process, he had become thoroughly familiar with the gulf region.

He also knew how to display the military's new technology to greatest effect. In one of the war's earliest televised briefings, Horner showed a video of smart bombs zapping key Iraqi facilities. "This is my counterpart's headquarters," he deadpanned as the world watched a huge Baghdad building being demolished with pinpoint precision.

Born in Davenport, Iowa, in 1936, Horner graduated from the University of Iowa in 1958 and immediately joined the Air Force. He earned an M.B.A. from the College of William and Mary in 1972 and attended the National War College in 1976. During his 30-plus years of service, he has won an array of awards and medals, including the Silver Star and Distinguished Flying Cross.

General Horner hunts, golfs, and flies a variety of Air Force planes for recreation. He and his wife, Mary Jo, a church organist also from Iowa, have three children.

In his command headquarters at Shaw, we discussed how to get a unique job done.

◆

Q. *You've said that to conduct the bombing campaign during the 1991 Gulf War you had to scrap previous plans. For a military man who drew up plans for three decades, wasn't that difficult?*

A. We didn't scrap all previous plans, only most of them. We'd long been studying warfare in that region, but warfare involving the Russians. Some of the "what ifs" apply to a war against a regional power like Iraq, but many don't. We had planned for working with other U.S. services, but not with other nations in a coalition. We had no sheet music for this contingency.

Q. *How do you know a plan will work?*

A. We don't. That's what makes military planning so tough. Like guys in business, we sit down and examine what could conceivably go wrong and try to make things better. That's why I treasure subordinates willing to step up and debate with me. I always encourage dissent— within reasonable bounds. Someone with thoughtful criticism could save lives.

Q. *Unlike your friends in business, you can't test-market your product in a realistic setting.*

A. That's why we were so anxious during those first hours of the Gulf War—in part because of a perception that the U.S. military couldn't do anything right after Vietnam and Desert One, the aborted rescue mission in Iran. We did our best, and I personally needed faith in God to get the job done.

Q. *But you didn't just rely on faith. You're known as a hard drillmaster, constantly demanding better plans, preparations, and practice.*

A. I give the troops the benefit of my experiences and make sure they've thought everything through. I've worked for guys who considered themselves the fountain of all knowledge. Nobody's that smart.

If a briefing is poorly presented, I make it mentally painful for the briefer so he won't waste my time again.

Q. *How do you manage that?*

A. I try to get somebody to see for himself how he could have done the job better. That way, the message sinks in. People are their own worst critics.

Q. *How did you coordinate the U.S. Army, Navy, Marines, and Air Force, and the nine air forces from coalition countries?*

A. Our regional buildup and preparations took four months, so we had time to anticipate most problems. Once we arrived at a common goal, folks began to cooperate and avoid doing silly things like playing power games.

Q. *But the French initially said they were going to do their own thing—to fly some places and not elsewhere.*

A. I had no quarrel with that. Within the central plan, I gave each nation the final say over what its forces would do. At one point, the French senior leader in the region wanted the French planes to fly only in support of French ground forces. I knew that the French Army was out of range of the French bases, so they often flew in support of U.S. Marines.

Q. *When he said that, did you say that his plans were impractical?*

A. No, I said they were okay. I knew where his ground forces were and knew that it would work out fine for us.

Q. *So you didn't kick and say that it was unreasonable to confine French air forces to support French ground troops?*

A. No, because it wasn't required. I knew that if it was a matter of life or death—if the U.S. Marines were getting overrun, for instance—the French planes were going to come to their aid. So why cause problems? I knew I was dealing with honest people. Besides, I knew that his instructions were out of touch with reality. The French air-force guy assured me, "We'll fly wherever you say we're needed." It all works out.

We were also lucky that the American leaders over there knew each other so well. I roomed with the Army leader, John Yeosock, in Saudi Arabia and knew the Navy chief, Stan Arthur. Walt Boomer of the Marine Corps is a quiet, studious guy who isn't given to charging over barbed wire to see how many bullets would hit the bodies of his heroic Marines. When you sit down with guys like that, you trust one another. No one has a hidden agenda.

Q. *Unlike people in other top jobs, though, you had to rely on others—in an extremely dangerous situation—whom you couldn't even help select. You were stuck with them.*

A. That's right. You take what you get and make the best of what you have. Besides, I could create a good environment, which is just as critical. If I trust the other fellows and they trust me, then anyone else coming into the situation soon finds that trusting is how it's done here. It is how things are done in the Arab world. If a Saudi gives his word, that's it. Arabs in general are reluctant to give their word. Sometimes it's hard to reach agreements, especially since they won't ever say "no" flatly. But once given, their word sticks.

Q. *Why did the Arab culture influence your thinking when you were organizing U.S. and coalition forces?*

A. Because I have to work with them too, especially with the Saudis. I'd been doing that for years, making a point always of being absolutely honest even if that was detrimental to my short-term objective.

This approach paid off. During the buildup and then the war, we could agree on a handshake. Whenever problems arose, we addressed them squarely. At first our military women driving vehicles in Saudi was a big deal for them. I said, "These women coming over here, they're going to die in defense of your country, and you're not going to let them drive a car? You've got to be kidding!" Then they said, "Oh. Okay."

Sometimes we tried to be too accommodating. The head of the Saudi air force came to me early on and asked why we suddenly called our chaplains "morale officers." He had gone to our War College and knew all about the U.S. military. I said that we didn't want to offend their culture. He wondered why it would offend the Saudis for us to have chaplains since they consider themselves among the most pious people on earth. We laughed at how we Americans had overreacted.

Q. *What were your big obstacles during the buildup?*

A. Just to get set. When I got off the plane in Riyadh in August, there were only six or seven of us to start defending Saudi Arabia.

Q. *With what?*

A. With whatever the Saudis then had and whatever we could get in fast. One night early on, I turned to the U.S. Army commander there and said, "We've got 20 Iraqi tank divisions up there. What have you got to stop them?" He reached in his pocket, pulled out his pocketknife, and said jokingly, "That's it."

Those were tough moments. Every day I wondered how to stop Saddam if he attacked Saudi Arabia. I wasn't sure he would attack, but it was my problem to stop him if he did. About mid-September we had enough forces in place to defeat him or deter him from coming into Saudi Arabia. Then we could refine our plans if we needed to attack him and eject his troops from Kuwait.

That was the main goal, besides crippling his nuclear, biological, and chemical capabilities. To do either or both, we first needed to seize control of the air. We knew Saddam wanted to inflict huge U.S. casualties, go on international television and stand on a heap of burned bodies.

Q. *To reignite our Vietnam syndrome?*

A. Yes. We had to avoid large casualties. That made sense from strategic and humanitarian points of view and was what President Bush wanted most. In all our discussions, the thing I came away with was President Bush's deep concern with the loss of life on both sides. Knowing his goals, and our capabilities against Saddam's, gave us the overall framework for our task.

So during the period from August to December 1990, we refined our plans if war should occur. We were sitting there with this indefiniteness, not knowing what the hell was going to happen. Our troops would ask, "How long am I going to be here?" Their spouses would write and ask if they were going to make it home for Christmas.

Suddenly we heard that people were popping up in Washington to say that we needed a rotation policy. Those of us who served in Vietnam were horrified. We didn't want a rotation policy. We wanted to get our forces there, get the job done, and get home. That's the American way. All this uncertainty and talk of rotation was tough for those of us planning the effort and preparing the troops.

One day I went down to Bateen, the old municipal airport in Abu Dhabi, United Arab Emirates, to visit a C-130 crew there. I saw this American kid wearing a shirt on which he had stencilled, BATEEN. HERE UNTIL VICTORY! He and his crew were living in tents but weren't complaining. They wanted to just get the job done. Seeing that kid's shirt stiffened my spine to stand up for no rotation policy.

Q. *What's wrong with a rotation policy?*

A. It takes away commitment. When a soldier's there for 90 days and gets out, he becomes a pieceworker. He doesn't own the business. You must give each person there a stake in the outcome to get a real commitment.

Q. *Between August and December 1990 you were planning the bombing campaign but didn't know if anything big was going to happen?*

A. That's right.

Q. *Then, all of a sudden, you have all these countries rolling in as part of a coalition.*

A. The coalition had been there all along. The Brits, French, Saudis, and Kuwaitis were in from the start. Everyone realized we had to fly off a single ATO [Air Tasking Order], even for peacetime training.

Q. *How did you put together the ATO every night? Two thousand flights daily? Getting the right munitions on the right planes going to the right targets by the right air forces?*

A. We had a decentralized system for people to execute a centralized plan. Defining our priorities gave us our target list. Each day we'd update the ATO based on intelligence inputs. We planned two days ahead of execution.

As for hitting Iraqi ground forces, I'd ask the Army, Marines, and coalition members what they wanted hit, and we'd put those targets on our list. We'd take the package to General Schwarzkopf every night and brief him: We're going to hit this, this, this. . . . We'd also give him a little feedback on how we'd done that day.

Schwarzkopf had his own Army plan and would tell us to hit this division here, hit that one there. Since we were going to hit them all anyway, I said fine. Obviously we wished to isolate the battlefield and keep the Republican Guard forces from escaping. We wanted them to stay put so we could destroy them where they were.

The approved plan would then go to the planners, who would calculate the air refueling requirements, bombing loads, etc. The printout of this Computer Automated Force Management System ran about 1,000 IBM sheets every day.

Q. *Where were you while this process was going on?*

A. We laid out the operation in three separate rooms in our offices in Riyadh. One was filled with maps and pictures and with intelligence guys and Army fellows scurrying around, freethinking, arguing, and coming up with notions on what to bomb during the next two days. Another room had a bunch of guys who looked like nerds, wearing glasses, typing into computers all our requirements and what to hit the next day. The third room looked like the *Daily Planet* room where Lois Lane worked. People there were executing the war and making changes to the plan as it was going on.

Each morning I'd go down to the planning room to talk to all those guys, then go to the second room and ask if all the computers were up and running, and then I'd go sit down and watch the war in the third room.

Q. *Do you still have a very centralized structure in the military?*

A. We've changed. Now we put decisions and responsibility at the lowest level possible. When I joined the Air Force, some officer would decide when a plane needed new tires. Hell, the guy that fixes the tires knows that better, so he decides now. We've got fewer and fewer regulations. When you have too many, nobody reads the damn things and nobody takes responsibility.

Q. *During war, do you think people rise to the occasion, performing better than ever?*

A. Yeah, but performance also relates to training. Vince Lombardi's teams played great on Sunday because they practiced on Thursday just as intensely. We too had very tough practices. The war was actually easier than the practices.

Q. *Fine, but Lombardi's teams knew there was a game on Sunday. Your guys didn't. How do you keep them pumped up when, after Vietnam, no one expected to go to war again?*

A. We in the Air Force don't have any trouble, since flying is beautiful and fun in itself. Even for the guy who loads bombs, it's beautiful and fun. And looking over the past few years—Grenada, Panama, Desert Storm—the question becomes not whether we'll ever go to war but when and where.

Pilots stay pumped up also by competition. So many of our exercises are competitions between planes or units. And leaders stress that people get killed if performance is not tops. That helps concentrate their minds.

Q. *Competing successfully is key to getting the job done. How transferable are other skills of yours to the nonmilitary world?*

A. I have no idea, but I think lots about that. I've found that the traits most needed for success are common sense, commitment, a sense of humor, and integrity. I learned how essential integrity is in the Pentagon. Often I was tempted to give some screaming general the answer he wanted. I decided instead to tell him the truth—always. That paid off. For once you compromise your integrity, you might as well compromise it all the time, because nobody's going to believe you.

Q. *There must have been times of tension and rivalry. How did you deal with that?*

A. By taking the high road. Once one of our services was planning to do something dysfunctional to the overall group. I knew that the three-star general in charge didn't know about it, so I sent him a message asking him to change things. He did.

Q. *All such issues were decided by you fellows in the field. You didn't have to go back to Washington with big decisions, which distinguished the Gulf War from the Vietnam War.*

A. Absolutely. General [Merrill] McPeak called me after he became Air Force chief of staff to say that even though we would be getting loads of calls from the Pentagon, we shouldn't answer them. That was a relief.

When Defense Secretary Dick Cheney came over and heard we were having too many visitors—requiring loads of logistical support and time—he put a stop to that. Unlike in Vietnam, we had clear, achievable strategic goals—not to fix Iraq but rather to expel its army from Kuwait. That we could do.

And we had detailed interest but not too much interference from Washington. When I briefed Secretary Cheney on taking out biological targets, our session was scheduled for 20 minutes. It went three and a half hours. It was open discussion without the attitude that he was the secretary and I was the subordinate. He made the key decisions, but after listening to what I had to say. So, unlike in Vietnam, the commanders in the Gulf War resisted getting sucked into doing something dumb simply to satisfy higher direction. I was prepared to retire rather than do something that would result in a needless loss of life.

Q. *Like what?*

A. Like create a buffer zone near the Iran border. One of my wing commanders called up one day and said, "Boss, I'm afraid we shot down two Iraqi planes over Iran. We were chasing them and going fast. There are no street signs, and we splashed two in Iran."

I called Schwarzkopf, who told General Colin Powell, who told Secretary Cheney. I braced myself for some lower-level, policy worry-widgets in Washington coming back and ordering us to implement a buffer zone. We had that in Vietnam. It's stupid. It costs lives, as it gives the enemy a sanctuary over part of their own country as well as over the neighboring countries.

I wasn't going to have a buffer zone. I was prepared to fight that, gently at first and then with everything I had. I was ready to quit, even though I love the Air Force. But that order never came.

Our generals in Vietnam lived in a different era, but there were times when they should have stood up. The U.S. military lost integrity then. And when you lose integrity, you lose everything.

Q. *What do you mean, you lost integrity?*

A. We reported hitting targets somewhere when we'd really hit them somewhere else. We jiggled figures on body counts and territory freed from the communists. In the Gulf War, we never reported anything we didn't absolutely know for sure, and we refused to give out estimates of enemy casualties. If we had, some reporter would have found something slightly different and called us liars. At first reporters were upset and accused us of hiding stuff. We didn't really.

Q. *Other Vietnam lessons learned?*

A. No gradualism. We planned to fight in the gulf as intensely and viciously as possible without giving Saddam any chance anywhere. We knew that gradualism in Vietnam stretched out the suffering of war. It's really immoral. War's immoral. If you decide you're going to take somebody's life, you can't fool around. You've got to go do it. War's a terrible thing to be in, but it's even worse if you're in halfway. That's why the air war in the gulf was so violent.

Q. *Looking back, what was the biggest obstacle you had?*

A. Dealing with uncertainty, initially. The weather was much worse than we anticipated and the Scud chase far more intensive than we planned. Hitting Scuds was important politically, since Israel and Saudi Arabia were in danger.

Q. *Your most intense moment?*

A. When the war started. There was a lot of anxiety, since we didn't know whether the Stealth bomber would work. Baghdad was a tough target, with guns on top of every building, rings of surface-to-air missiles everywhere. The Iraqis had a first-rate air force.

Q. *Were you surprised that the president said "go" on January 16th of last year?*

A. I knew in November, when our air plan was finished and we briefed the president, that we'd probably go.

Q. *That may have been obvious to you, but it wasn't obvious to the rest of us in Washington or to Egyptian president Hosni Mubarak or the Saudi king or most others who figured that Saddam would back down, even at the last minute.*

A. It was obvious to anybody who'd watched Saddam build up his defenses and add more divisions in Kuwait. If he intended to withdraw, he wouldn't have done that.

Q. *Why couldn't you use smart weapons and knock off Saddam himself?*

A. We didn't target him personally, but we did target key command and control facilities where he should have been. Besides, some of his bunkers were very deep and well constructed. Others were in residential areas, and we didn't bomb those. We knew at one point that he was using Winnebagos, or mobile units, as command posts. So when we'd come across one of those, it got special attention.

Q. *So why didn't you hit him?*

A. He did get shot up once, when our F-16s destroyed a convoy he was in. We hit half the cars, but not the right half.

Q. *Do we know he was in it?*

A. We didn't know then. We do know now. We killed some of his nice bodyguards.

Q. *How did Saddam do as commander?*

A. Lousy. He chose to keep complete command, so that his forces couldn't decide anything themselves. That was his principal weakness. Second was his ignorance of modern air power. He didn't have a clue. We flew in just one day what he faced in eight years of war with Iran. He lacked air experience and lacked anybody who would teach him.

Q. *The only other disappointment Americans had was in the high casualty rate from friendly fire. What went wrong?*

A. Our losses were so low, and the war so intense, that the percentage of friendly-fire losses was high. Out of the 35 armored vehicles the Army lost, 27 were hit by the Army itself. That's terrible, but the good news is that a total of only 35 were hit.

Q. *How about from the air?*

A. We lost very few troops or matériel from the air—maybe four wrong hits. We took extraordinary measures. Still, the lethality of modern air weapons means that we need solutions to this problem.

Q. *Because the air war was so antiseptic, will it tempt future U.S. leaders to be trigger-happy?*

A. I do worry about someone considering war a reasonable way of solving problems. That scares me. People saw this war on television as sterile, mechanistic, technological—my laser-guided bombs against his munitions factories. I saw it as our guys going through a hail of lead, knowing that surface-to-air missiles were being fired at them, and having sweat run down their necks.

I don't want Americans going around saying, "Yeah, we sure kicked the shit out of those guys." I'm happy that Americans came to feel good about themselves, to gain confidence by the Gulf War. They feel we did the right thing and a good job. That makes us awfully happy.

EVERY 22 SECONDS, SOMETHING QUITE UNEVENTFUL
HAPPENS SOMEWHERE IN THE WORLD.

A Citation takes off or lands safely every 22 seconds. The aircraft's safety record is even more remarkable considering there are nearly 2,000 of them in the world's largest fleet of business jets.

In aviation, the Collier Trophy is the highest tribute to excellence. The trophy was created in 1911, but 75 years went by before it was given to honor a business aircraft company.

The Citation's unmatched safety record is why that company is Cessna.

The Sensible Citations

Chapter Five

THE POWER
OF PERSUASION

"A h, the tombstone question!" Sandra Day O'Connor said when asked during her 1981 Senate confirmation hearings how she'd like to be remembered. "I hope it says, 'Here lies a good judge.' I hope I am remembered as the first woman who served on the Supreme Court." She will surely be remembered as both.

Born in El Paso, Texas, in 1930, Sandra Day grew up on a remote Arizona ranch without electricity and learned early to ride a horse, drive a truck, and round up cattle. Her rural origins foretold little of her future.

She excelled at school, graduating from Stanford with a B.A. in economics in 1950 and a law degree two years later. It was while working on the *Law Review* that she met John Jay O'Connor III, whom she married in 1952 and with whom she's reared three sons.

Hard as it is to believe, following her graduation O'Connor was spurned by major law firms: they didn't hire women. Instead she embarked on a lifetime largely of public service, which has taken her into each branch of government: executive appointments as a government attorney in California and Arizona; legislative work in the Arizona Senate, where she became the first female majority leader in any state legislature; and judicial service, initially on the Superior Court in Phoenix and then on the Arizona Court of Appeals, where she was serving in July 1981 when President Reagan nominated her to the Supreme Court.

SANDRA DAY O'CONNOR
Associate Justice, U.S. Supreme Court

Justice O'Connor works herself and her law clerks hard, including weekends and most holidays, but she refuses to be cloistered in the Court. She has formed an exercise class consisting of women who work at the Supreme Court, and she plays many sports, especially tennis and golf.

She also speaks out on women's issues. Recently she told an audience at Washington University that women rarely become senior executives, because of "blatant sex discrimination and the widespread belief that women are unfit for power positions."

The justice is strikingly poised and dignified. We sat in her chambers, lined from floor to ceiling with law reference books, as she told how to get the job done.

◆

Q. *Have you suffered professionally as a woman?*

A. I've been through a total change in my life span. When I left law school in 1952 . . .

Q. *As number one in your class at Stanford?*

A. No, [Chief Justice] William Rehnquist was in my law-school class, and he was clearly number one. But I did well.

Anyway, at that time none of the major California firms had ever hired a woman as a lawyer.

Q. *What were you told?*

A. Just that—they had never hired a woman as a lawyer and never intended to do so. One firm ended up giving me a job offer as a legal secretary. That wasn't really what I had in mind.

Q. *Women today have a totally different situation, obviously.*

A. I went to law school when only a handful of women attended. Today most law schools have 50 percent women. And law firms around the country actively recruit women lawyers today. While they still aren't represented in sufficient numbers as judges and partners in law firms, the number of women has increased year by year.

Q. *So for you, being a woman has not been a major obstacle.*

A. Being turned down by law firms redirected me into public service, which worked out happily for me. But like other women, I faced some disadvantages, and I'm pleased to have been able to help correct some of those as I went along.

Nonetheless, women, even today, face difficulties men don't face. For women who seek a career, the plain, hard fact of the matter is they will spend much more time as the primary caregiver for the children, home, and family than men in a career. So women have to make hard choices between having children, or when to have children, and a career. In some occupations women face the so-called mommy factor, or a glass ceiling that puts a lid on how high they can rise.

Q. *Obviously that didn't happen to you. But your career has required a lot of flexibility. For instance, being a politician in the Arizona legislature draws upon different skills than the job of Supreme Court justice.*

A. It surely does. I had long been interested in state government. With considerable difficulty I finally landed a job in the state attorney general's office. My clients included the state treasurer and auditor, who dealt with all state expenditures. They had a finger in every pie, and so did I. I enjoyed that job, probably more than any other I've ever had.

After that assignment a vacancy opened in the Arizona State Senate, and I decided to go for it. At first I doubted whether I could do the job. I lacked any legislative experience, and I didn't know how that body operated. But because of my legal training and state experience, I was immediately made chairman of the State, County, and Municipal Affairs Committee.

Q. *You walked in as chairman?*

A. Yes, which was unusual and exciting, because this committee had a say on most aspects of state government. Since the Republicans held a majority in both legislative chambers, we could offer legislation fully expecting that it would be passed.

I knew what I wanted to accomplish in that job. For instance, I wished to review state laws that contained gender discrimination. At that time Arizona gave the husband sole management and control of community property in a marriage, to the obvious disadvantage of married women. Happily this was a change I was able to draft and get passed.

Q. *What does it take to get the job done in the legislative branch?*

A. I thought hard at first about what I really needed to focus on. I asked, "What do we need to do to make our state better? What are our big problems and how can we develop sensible solutions to them?"

I'd gather information about a particular problem and see whether proposed solutions were floating around anywhere. I was never restricted in what I could examine or whom I could ask. I collected written material but could also pick up the telephone and get the most knowledgeable people around to comment on any given issue. That was one of the best parts of the job.

Q. *If they're that knowledgeable, don't those people usually have an ax to grind?*

A. A university professor might not, but often, yes, you end up talking to people on both sides of an issue. Then you try to draw your own conclusions on what approach makes most sense. And you have to gauge whether you can gain enough statewide support for that measure to become enacted.

Q. *The first part of the job sounds cerebral, almost judicial—setting your priorities, figuring out what the main problems are, talking to people about solutions. The second part sounds more familiar—a great deal of politicking and schmoozing.*

A. Yes, it comes down to that when you're trying to get a measure enacted. You need to have enough personal contacts with members to gain their support for measures that you think are terribly important but that they might not.

Q. *Did you have to trade many votes for dams and power projects?*

A. Not directly. I didn't want to do that, didn't like it. Nonetheless, I found myself under subtle pressure to accommodate those who had helped me, so their support wouldn't be a one-way street. That isn't terribly pleasant, though it's part of politics.

I was a nitpicker in the legislature because I cared what every statute said. If I found a mistake, I wanted it corrected whether it was my bill or someone else's. I considered that a special obligation, since there were very few lawyers then serving in the legislature, which is unusual.

Q. *What were some of the toughest parts of the job?*

A. People throughout Arizona who wanted something done in the legislature would approach me to push their ideas. They often did so by flattery, or attempted flattery. Now this is not a very healthy way to live. Many politicians begin to believe such flattery. I was happy both to have served in the legislative branch and to have given it up. To stay there too long is dangerous.

Q. *To one's ego?*

A. Yes. The flattery comes from everywhere.

After three years I was elected majority leader of the state Senate, the first woman so elected in the U.S. That was terribly exciting, but it brought me a new array of problems. For then I had to persuade colleagues to go along with the majority's program. That could be touchy. In our Senate of 30 members, Republicans had only 16 seats. So I always needed every vote. Any one Republican could hold me up for some outrageous reason, which was frustrating.

Q. *What techniques did you find were most persuasive?*

A. That varied with the individual. I tried to learn what would motivate a particular legislator to support a particular measure. It could be one phone call from a key constituent or help with a legislative proposal.

Q. *How many of those skills or techniques do you use as a Supreme Court justice?*

A. None. This is a totally different setting and branch of government. On an appellate court, like the Supreme Court, decisions don't depend on personalities or egos or working on somebody else's special interest. The power of persuasion here comes from clarity and strength of reasoning, from the quality of ideas one puts forward. There's no behind-the-scenes lobbying. Justices work hard to write a decision that persuades the other members to adopt that view.

Q. *In your weekly meetings—held without any staff, just the nine of you— is there no attempt to convince other justices of your position?*

A. No, it just doesn't work that way. Oral conferences are not the occasion to try to persuade others. By then justices have invested lots of time on any particular case, and most have already developed a position before we get together to discuss it. The weekly conference is an opportunity to hear other views, not to persuade others of the strength of your position. That occurs at the writing stage.

Q. *But have there been occasions when you've heard another justice and changed your mind?*

A. Of course. But again, it's generally when an opinion gets written that a justice changes a viewpoint or approach.

Q. *Has the Court always been like that, or was there a time when one justice who felt strongly about an issue would trade his vote with another justice who felt strongly about a different issue?*

A. I don't know, but nothing like that happens now.

Q. *So yours is really a cerebral existence.*

A. Very much so.

Q. *Nothing like depending upon personal relations, as you did in the Arizona legislature.*

A. We're very cordial and respectful here, but each judge essentially does his or her own work.

Q. *When you entered the Arizona legislature, you had specific things you wished to accomplish. Did that happen when you entered the Supreme Court?*

A. No. I certainly didn't come here wanting to achieve anything specific. I did find that there was much to learn. I worked hard to grasp the essential mechanics of this job, which took me a long time. The only thing I initially wanted to achieve was to do a good job on each and every case that came along.

Q. *What does that take?*

A. A lot of reading, of concentration, of thinking.

Q. *So in the decade you've been here, the tools you use to get this job done are basically intellectual.*

A. Yes. This is an academic job, in large measure. I spend an enormous amount of time reading and evaluating the positions put forward. I analyze past cases and the record of the case before me. Then I try to write a decision that's persuasive.

Q. *The job is more written than oral.*

A. Oh yes. The persuasion takes place on paper. A justice needs to see exactly what's being argued.

Q. *You hire four law clerks, who fill important but fairly invisible positions in government. Tell us about their selection.*

A. We get applications, each of us, though usually from the same pool. Applicants tend to apply to all chambers.

Q. *How many are you talking about? Thousands?*

A. No, maybe 300 or so. The most talented young lawyers in the country want to clerk here, but normally we don't hire any straight out of law school. Most spend at least a year clerking at a lower-level court first.

I review the applications during the spring. I'll set aside maybe 50 files of people who strike me as the most promising. Then I'll go through that stack with much more care. I'll read their references and try to winnow it down to just a handful.

I typically interview a few more than I can hire. That's the worst part of the process, since I usually like them all. I don't want to turn anyone down after I've interviewed the person. To do that is very painful.

Q. *What do you look for?*

A. Tremendous intellectual capacity and strength. Objectivity. I don't want someone coming with an ax to grind or coming to put a personal imprint on things. I look for someone who can be compatible and congenial with me and the other clerks in this chamber and throughout the building. It's critical to avoid people who are abrasive or have personal problems. We need their full, undivided attention to work for a year, without any interruption or internal dissension.

And I look for diversity of backgrounds and experiences. A high percentage of applicants have advanced degrees in other fields, which is beneficial. I had one clerk who taught astrophysics before going to law school, another with a Ph.D. in chemistry, one who was a tenured engineering professor at MIT, and so on. I have found that very interesting.

Q. *Do you assign them the cases, or do you . . .*

A. They sort that out themselves. I like to have one law clerk do additional research on every case argued here, but otherwise they devise their own system of dividing up the work.

Q. *Do they make recommendations?*

A. Sure. They tell me how they analyze a case. We discuss it, but I decide it.

Q. *How?*

A. That's a very personal thing. I sit down by myself with my notes and files and the briefs and then reach a conclusion.

Q. *Does that come early in the process or late?*

A. Late. Just before we go into our oral conference discussion.

Q. *Is that agonizing for you?*

A. Sure, though some decisions come more easily. Some cases are decided by drawing very fine lines, which makes them extremely difficult to resolve.

Q. *Chief Justice Charles Evans Hughes told William O. Douglas when he entered the Supreme Court, "At the constitutional level, where we work, 90 percent of any decision is emotional. The rational part of us supplies the reasons for supporting our predilections."*

A. I don't share that perception at all. Not at all. We make an enormous effort to craft a sensible, workable rule to resolve a particular issue in a way that will be useful to others faced with the same or a similar problem. While we have personal preferences, we don't write our decisions to satisfy those preferences.

Q. *You're known as one of the most disciplined of justices and of individuals. Is that your nature or what the job demands?*

SHORTLY AFTER FLYING IN A CITATION, HUNDREDS OF PASSENGERS HAVE GONE ON TO BECOME CELEBRATED SPORTS HEROES.

In 1987 and again in 1991, hundreds of Citation owners volunteered their aircraft, pilots and fuel to airlift thousands of athletes to the International Special Olympics Games. The airlift was organized by Cessna. But the generous cooperation of Citation owners brought it to reality.

When we asked Citation owners to help these special people celebrate life in an unforgettable way, they didn't think twice.

They did it twice.

THE SENSIBLE CITATIONS

Cessna
A Textron Company

A. I don't think I'm any more disciplined than the others here, but I've always been able to concentrate well. I grew up on a ranch in a very remote area that had no school. So I was sent off to live with my grandmother in El Paso from kindergarten on.

My grandmother was a wonderful woman, quite devoted to me, but she talked incessantly. If she was awake, she was talking. To get my homework done, I had to learn to listen lightly so her talking wouldn't break my concentration. I have never been easily distracted since then. I can focus on what I have to do, even with a lot of commotion around me. I'm grateful to my grandmother for that, among other things.

It also helped me to take a speed-reading course, which I did after I was married and living in Phoenix. I figured that would help me in my work, and it did. As a legislator I had to read vast quantities of material. But I've never needed speed-reading more than as a justice, since we have such vast amounts to read and digest.

Q. *But can a justice read quickly and carefully at the same time?*

A. It depends on what I'm reading. Sometimes I have to slow down, but a lot of material I can scan. Some petitions for certiorari—requests to be heard and decided by this Court—and portions of briefs I need only glance through.

Q. *Talking about petitions of certiorari, you must get thousands a year. Do you decide ahead of time that you'd like to have a case on such and such and go searching for one?*

A. The Supreme Court is a uniquely reactive institution. It reacts to the interests and legal concerns of those outside the Court, to a legislature or public official, or to private disputes of litigants. We don't create these cases. We don't go seeking them.

Q. *But there's such a variety.*

A. Yes, indeed. But our main concern here is not error correction. It's trying to develop a reasonably uniform and consistent body of federal law. We're most interested in petitions for certiorari that present an important issue of federal law that will probably keep reoccurring across the country, and one on which lower courts have reached conflicting opinions.

Out of all the applications we receive, only a small percentage fit these criteria. So we end up taking only about 150 cases a year out of more than 5,000 petitions. We are very selective. And if we happen to miss a key issue the first time or two around, it will come back. We can count on that.

Q. *How does it feel to have a job for the rest of your life?*

A. Strange. That's unusual for me. Until now I've done each job for under 10 years and then made a change. It's allowed me to have the most marvelous experiences going through life.

Well, I don't do that anymore. I'm here to stay for the long haul.

So I approach this job a little more slowly, using a little more care.

The other thing that's different here is that once I've decided an issue, it's hard to change views. When a related problem arises, I look back and read what I've already written.

Q. *Can't you just say that times have changed or that your mind has changed?*

A. Yes, you can, but that's not a very attractive thing to do. We don't do that often. We leave footprints as we walk through the job, and each of us is acutely aware of those footprints.

Q. *What footprints make for a great justice?*

A. That clarity of thought that enables a justice to see the crucial issues and the solutions, to draw analogies, and to see the effects of what's proposed. After deciding all that, it takes a keen capacity to write the decision up in a way that's persuasive and clear.

Q. *Drawing upon all your experiences, what does it take to get the job done in life?*

A. To work hard and not expect things to come easily. You must learn discipline. You need to learn how to get along well with people, because nearly all positions depend on that. And for your own peace of mind, it's good to have a sense of humor. That makes life so much more pleasant.

THE MEN WHO MANAGE CESSNA AIRCRAFT COMPANY HAVE HAD ONE THING IN COMMON EVER SINCE THEY WERE BOYS.

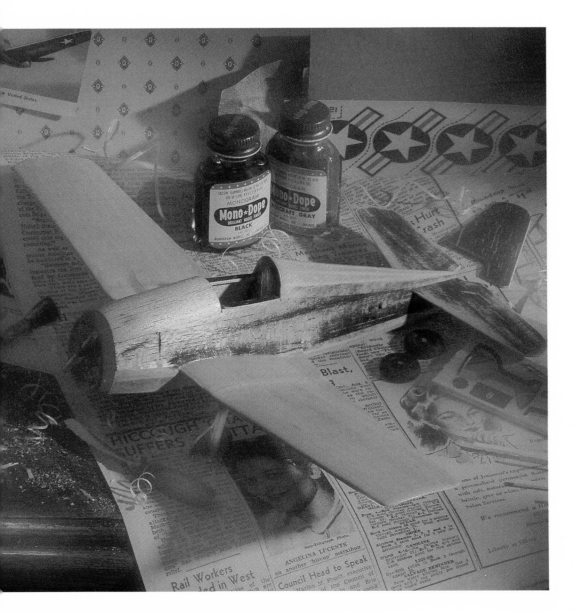

You could call it a lifelong fascination with aviation. You might even call it an obsession. Whatever it is, Cessna's top executives have never outgrown it. All of them are active pilots.

Some would say you don't have to be a pilot to build a good airplane. And they're probably right. But to build a great airplane, we believe it takes something beyond mere aerodynamics and aluminum.

We believe it takes a little passion.

THE SENSIBLE CITATIONS

Cessna
A Textron Company

Chapter Six

JUST DO IT

At 18 John H. Johnson was on welfare. By 27 he was a millionaire. Now over 70, the founder, chairman, and CEO of Johnson Publishing Company manages a publishing and cosmetics empire with annual revenues of $250 million. He is America's foremost black publisher, marking his 50th anniversary in the business this year.

Johnson is pleased, but he's not complacent. He runs his empire with diligence, inexhaustible energy, and a smattering of superstition. He has founded all his publications in November because he considers it his lucky month: *Ebony*, the monthly *Life* look-alike for black readers, in 1945; *Jet*, a *TV Guide*-size weekly newsmagazine, in 1951; and *Ebony Man*, similar to *GQ*, in 1985. Johnson got his first break in, yes, November 1942. At age 24 he launched *Negro Digest* with a $500 loan, using his mother's furniture as collateral. Gertrude Johnson Williams prayed a lot, heard the Lord, and told her son, "Go ahead."

Gertrude Johnson, widowed when Johnson was 8, wanted her son well educated. But Johnson's birthplace, Arkansas City, Arkansas, lacked any schooling for blacks beyond the eighth grade. So mother and son moved to Chicago, living briefly on welfare until she found a job.

The young Johnson edited the school newspaper and was elected class president at Du Sable High School on Chicago's South Side. In 1936, when the school's top graduates attended a lunch whose keynote speaker was Harry H. Pace, the prominent black president of Supreme

JOHN H. JOHNSON
Chairman and chief executive officer, Johnson Publishing Company

Life Insurance Company, Johnson so impressed Pace that he hired him as a part-time office boy.

Next, Johnson entered the University of Chicago but stayed only two years. Before long, he concocted the idea of an upbeat magazine for blacks, *Negro Digest*. A host of problems soon arose. When Chicago distributors refused to put the new publication on newsstands, Johnson got his friends to request copies time and again until the distributors felt obliged to accept the magazine. This same ploy—repeated in Detroit, New York, and Philadelphia—successfully launched the magazine. Within a year *Negro Digest* was selling 50,000 copies monthly.

Johnson was off and running. In addition to his publications, he subsequently launched two lines of beauty products, a book-publishing house, a travel service, a fashion fair, and several syndicated television shows.

Today Johnson's publications reach more than half of all black American adults. *Ebony*, with a circulation of 1.8 million and a readership of 8.7 million, has been number one in circulation among blacks since its launch 47 years ago. *Jet* has some 8.5 million readers weekly. And both magazines reflect Johnson's message of excellence and hope for black Americans. He likes to quote Adlai Stevenson's comment about Eleanor Roosevelt: "She would rather light candles than curse the darkness."

Running his empire is hard work, but Johnson considers it more fun than taking vacations. "People go on vacation to do exactly what they would like to do," he says. "By that definition, I'm on vacation all the time." He describes himself as "a hands-on, hands-in, hands-wrapped-around manager." He still signs every company check himself.

He and his wife, Eunice, who have been married for 50 years, lost a son to sickle cell anemia in 1981. Their daughter, Linda Johnson Rice, is currently the publishing company's chief operating officer.

In his swanky Michigan Avenue headquarters on Chicago's lake front, Johnson explained how to get the job done.

◆

Q. *When you started out, did you know what you were going to do?*

A. No. You can't go into a room and come out with a great idea for a business. You have to look for opportunities. I found mine when my boss asked me to scan publications and summarize events in the black community. I'd tell friends about these articles and they'd say, "Gee, that sounds interesting. How can I get it?" I knew about *Reader's Digest* and found an opportunity for *Negro Digest*.

Q. *But others had the same idea and fell on their faces.*

A. I'm not good at falling on my face.

Q. *Okay, but didn't it scare you to realize that your idea was no new idea at all? It had been tried and failed.*

A. Sure I was scared. I've been scared with every new move I make. But I believed I could start that magazine.

Q. *Why? Those others felt that way too.*

A. There was a clear need for it. Those who preceded me didn't take their direction from the marketplace. They produced black intellectual magazines dealing primarily with the race problem. They did not, and perhaps could not, tell people how to solve that problem. Folks read the magazines and became disillusioned.

My mother taught me faith, to believe in things unseen. She said, "Son, if you believe you can do it, you can do it."

Q. *Still, loads of people have the same faith, from their mothers or whomever, and just go from dream to dream.*

A. But I was 24 years old and didn't know that many others had failed. Maybe had I known then what I know now, I wouldn't have done it. Maybe I succeeded because I didn't know I could fail. A feasibility study would have shown I couldn't do it, but I didn't know about feasibility studies. Anyway, I knew that people wanted the product. Remember, few positive articles about blacks ran in the white media then. I figured that if I could assemble those articles in one little packet, people would buy it.

Q. *But blacks didn't have much money to buy magazines.*

A. You underestimate the black economic potential. People always say blacks are poor, but I wasn't intending to sell to poor blacks. I wanted to sell to blacks who could afford magazines. So I decided to send out letters and ask people to send in advance subscriptions. But before that, I had to figure out what would make people buy this thing, still unpublished. That's the key to business—getting inside the other person's mind. Why would anyone send me $2 for a magazine they'd never heard of or seen?

Q. *And that didn't exist.*

A. Not yet. But I concluded that, more than anything else, blacks wanted respect. If all day long people are putting you down and calling you nigger and refusing to serve you in restaurants and turning you away from hotels, it's demoralizing. Our women couldn't even try on hats in department stores.

So I thought, "These people want to feel good about themselves." I finally wrote my letter saying—and I remember it as if it were yesterday—"A good friend of yours told me about you." I wanted to make them feel that somebody had recommended them. "They told me you are a person who is well thought of in the community, that you like to keep abreast of current events. Because of this recommendation, I'm offering you a charter subscription to *Negro Digest*, provided you send $2 (by a certain date) because the price will go up after that." Around 3,000 people sent me the money. With that $6,000, I was off.

Q. *How did you get the mailing list?*

A. From the insurance company where I worked. That kind man Mr. Pace, who hired me without having any real job for me, gave me 20,000 names of his premium customers.

Q. *All black?*

A. All black and hard working, or they couldn't have paid for their insurance.

Q. *So you flattered them, you got them all puffed up when they read your letter.*

A. Selling is emotional, not mechanical. You have to touch people, to get down deep, to give them something they're striving for. You have to know what moves a person or group. I've been known to take months to sell one person. When approaching a prospect, I'm looking for an edge, an opening. I want to connect with that person by talking about what he wants—not about what I want.

And I have to do investigative reporting. Years ago I wanted to get my cosmetics into Neiman-Marcus, the premium department store. If I could get the line in there, other stores would follow. So I visited the Dallas store and noticed it had very few, if any, black customers. I finally got in to see the head man by saying that I wanted to talk about how he could get more black customers.

I offered him our cosmetic line on an exclusive basis for five years. I told him that when black women came in to buy Fashion Fair, they'd see other products and he'd have new customers. He said, "That sounds pretty good." So I sold him by thinking about what he wanted.

Q. *Your first big break for magazine advertising came with Zenith. What happened?*

A. *Ebony* had been out for six months and was about to fail. It was a big success, since black people wanted it—going from 25,000 copies to 200,000—but I couldn't sell advertising. I tried everything, including white salesmen. Nothing worked, so I decided to try selling ads myself.

I'm thinking hard then about who to approach. I notice one day that my mother has a Zenith radio. All blacks seem to have Zenith radios. So I figure, I'll try Zenith!

I write the company president, Commander Eugene McDonald, who writes back "no," since he doesn't handle advertising. I'm 25 and not sophisticated about business, so I'm thinking, "What would he handle? He must handle policy!" I write him back and ask to talk to him about policy.

"Okay," he writes back, "I'll give you an appointment, but I still believe you want to talk about advertising. And if you talk about that, I'll ask you to leave my office."

So now I have an appointment to talk to somebody who says that the one thing I want to talk about, I can't talk about. Okay, what can I do?

I decide to learn enough about the guy to keep the conversation going. Maybe we'll end up talking about advertising. So I look him up in *Who's Who* and find that he was an explorer and had been on a North Pole expedition. Then I learn that a black guy named Matthew Henson went with Admiral Peary on his expedition to the pole and had written a book. He was still alive and living in New York, so I get a New York buddy to have Henson autograph his book for the Zenith president, and I write a story for *Ebony* on Henson.

While writing this I learn a big lesson from Henson—that in order to succeed you must make yourself indispensable. The night before Peary took his last run to the pole, all the distinguished white scientists wanted to be there when he raised the flag. Peary paced the floor and finally said, "Gentlemen, I can only take one other member of this expedition, four Eskimos, and six dogs. I know you're all anxious to go with me, but I've got to take Henson. I can't make it without him."

Henson, you see, knew the Eskimo language, the only language the dogs understood. He had made himself indispensable.

Q. *You wrote the story in* Ebony *just for your Zenith appointment?*

A. Yes. And on a hot day in July in 1946, I go to Zenith and see some snowshoes by the door of the president's office. He says, "Young man, do you see those snowshoes?" I say, "Yes, Commander." He says, "They were given to me by a black man named Matthew Henson. He's as good as any two white men I know." I say, "That's great, Commander." He says, "Did you ever hear of Henson?" I say, "Yes," and he says, "I hear Matt wrote some kind of book." I say, "I just happen to have a copy, Commander, and Matt's autographed it for you."

The Commander looks at the book, and now he's getting mighty pleased. He says, "Well, I understand you've got a magazine. If it's any kind of magazine, you would have done something on a guy like Matt." I say, "I just happen to have a copy here, Commander." He asks to see it and runs across my article about Henson.

He turns to me and says, "I really don't see why we shouldn't advertise in a magazine like this!" I say, "Well, I don't see any reason why you shouldn't either, Commander." I'm getting mighty pleased now.

He pushes a button and the advertising manager, a guy named Mackie, walks in and bows. The Commander asks, "Why aren't we in *Ebony*?" By then I'd been trying to see Mackie for months, but Mackie's cool here. "We're considering it, Commander," he says.

The Commander asks me about the magazine, and I explain that we try to stress the brighter side of black life, to inspire black people to achieve, and to write about what the races have in common rather than their differences. He asks how I am doing, and I say, "Well, I'm not doing well. I'm having trouble selling advertising."

He offers to call up some friends and see what he can do to help. So while I'm sitting there, he calls up the chairman of Swift, of Quaker Oats, Elgin Watch, and Armour. "I have a young black fellow in my office with a good story to tell. He's soliciting advertising." This was the turning point for me.

Q. *Your whole business is selling—advertising, the magazine, black life . . .*

A. Yes. I want people to feel good about themselves. We feature success. When someone's making it, we rush to do a story and always ask how he or she did it. Even today I'm curious how a successful person does what he does.

Q. *What common traits have you found?*

A. You have to believe in yourself in order to convince others. I got over my fear of public speaking by practicing before the mirror day after day. I'd tell myself, "John Johnson, you can do it. You can do it. You can do it!"

You have to prepare for opportunities that are not yet available. Jackie Robinson had to be a qualified player before he could get in the big leagues. Colin Powell had to be a qualified soldier before any black could become chairman of the Joint Chiefs. Thurgood Marshall had to be a good lawyer before a black could go onto the Supreme Court.

Never burn bridges behind you. I owed my first printer $14,000 when I had to switch printers. I told him, "I can't pay you now, but I'll pay you as soon as I can." I did, and he's still my friend.

Q. *You're known for having good people around. How do you hire?*

A. I look for people who will work as hard as I do. Not all people who work hard succeed, but all people who succeed work hard.

References aren't that helpful anymore, since people are afraid to say what they think about an employee. But I look for job skills and people skills.

Q. *Is your batting average good?*

A. Very good now. Before, when white companies first began hiring black professionals, they'd find that I had the only ones skilled in marketing, advertising, and journalism. They stole them from me. That hurt. So one day I sat down and listed the 30 or so people I needed to survive. I put the list on an easel near my desk. Every morning I'd look it over and say, "Gee, what can I do today to make these people so satisfied that they'll never leave me?"

To answer that I had to understand each of them. I never knew them before—who had children, what their aspirations were. I began to take them out to lunch. I learned that some wanted promotions, others more money, better titles. I told them to call me whenever they had a problem. I gave them whatever they wanted.

After that I never lost a single person. *Ebony's* executive editor has been here 38 years; *Jet's* executive editor has been here for 39 years; my former secretary, who is now the company general counsel, and the head of personnel—both have been here more than 30 years.

Q. *How do you motivate them?*

A. Bonuses and especially by saying thank you. I write little notes to tell them what a great job they did on something. I even thank the kitchen help. When we have big entertainers come by—Stevie Wonder, Lena Horne, Sidney Poitier—I go into the kitchen and thank the staff for the great job they did.

Q. *That's nice, but they'd probably like to meet the stars even more.*

A. Yeah, so I take the stars in there, too.

Q. *How do you fire somebody?*

A. Face to face. You need to warn the person first and say, "Unless

PERHAPS THE MOST IMPORTANT THING WE BUILD AT THIS CESSNA PLANT IS HUMAN POTENTIAL.

A year ago, this Cessna worker was considered unemployable. Lacking skills and education, she and her children lived on welfare checks.

But a new program, initiated by Cessna Aircraft Company, changed all that. The program provides job training for the undereducated. It gives each person a basic skill, a means to make a living, and a source of pride.

Graduates of the program now build high-quality parts for Cessna and, at the same time, something even more valuable. Better lives for themselves.

THE SENSIBLE CITATIONS

Cessna
A Textron Company

you improve (such and such), I'll have to terminate your services." Then you write a letter confirming what you've said. If they continue to do whatever, you dismiss them in person.

Q. *When you give a warning, do most people change so that you don't have to fire them?*

A. Oh yes, 75 percent. I've also learned not to overpromote people. This is my big weakness. Early on I took a young woman in charge of the machine for circulation lists and made her circulation manager. Suddenly she fired everybody in the department, and so I had to fire her instead. Next day she came by and said, "Mr. Johnson, you should've known I wasn't qualified for that job. I got scared. I reacted badly."

She asked me if she had done well in her job before, and I said yes. She said, "You're a fair man. I'm asking for my old job back. I'll personally apologize to each person I fired. If they accept my apology, will you take me back?" I said sure. That lady worked another 35 years in that job. I gave her raises but kept her at that machine.

In the early days I was too eager to promote people. If I had an extraordinarily good writer, I'd make him or her a managing editor. That was a mistake, because I was asking my best writers to manage people who didn't write as well. I finally found other titles, like senior editor, to enable the writer to keep writing but to receive recognition and more money.

Q. *Have you stayed within the black community for your hires?*

A. I first hired many whites because blacks didn't know these jobs. But I trained blacks since I felt a mission to bring blacks into these fields.

Q. *Can you be accused of reverse discrimination?*

A. No. Johnson Publishing was born integrated. We had a white executive editor at least 20 years before any white corporation had a black middle manager, not to mention a top executive. That tradition still lives here. I never refuse to hire a qualified person of any race. In fact, no white person is turned away unless I see the application first. I do that because people tend to hire people like themselves. I don't want blacks only hiring blacks.

When I hired my first white employee, folks here wrote a petition asking me to do three things: to start the white at the bottom, like they start us; to have him sit in the back of the office, where whites put blacks; and to not allow the white fellow to go out with our black girls, because whites don't want us dating their white girls.

I read the petition and said, "Let's compromise. We'll sit him in the middle of the office. I can't start him at the bottom but won't start him at the top either. And I can't speak to the black-girl issue. Our black girls will have to decide that." Everything worked out fine.

When people get to know each other, racial stereotypes go away. We now have several white people, including a vice-president in charge of the computer division. About 50 black women work for him. They don't think of him as white, just as a caring, considerate person. There's little turnover in his department.

Q. *Is the work ethic weaker among blacks than whites?*

A. It's weak everywhere. This is a generation thing. When I call white friends to complain about some black workers, they say, "I've got loads of white workers I'll trade with you." Younger people aren't as committed to the work ethic. They expect more from society than we did. They're not willing to pay their dues.

Q. *It's no worse in the black community?*

A. It might even be a bit better, because we've had enough knocks. When we get a job, we want to keep it. I felt that way when I got the *Negro Digest* going. I wanted to keep it going. But I didn't know anything about the publishing business.

I was reading a book about Henry Luce and one day decided to call him up. I got his secretary on the line and said, "I'm starting a new black magazine and don't know anything about it. I don't want any money. I don't want anything from Mr. Luce except some guidance and recommendations. I wonder if I could meet with him for a few minutes." She called back and said, "Yes, he'll see you."

So I went in and he was very gracious. I was particularly interested in circulation, and he sent a little note to the head of that division. My people and I met with his circulation people, and they told us that blue envelopes get better response than red ones, that kind of thing. I did the same thing with Gardner Cowles at *Look* magazine. I took my people to Des Moines to learn from his people.

Q. *That was clever, piggybacking on their years of experience.*

A. That was the only way for me to find out. There weren't any courses on circulation or on how to be a publisher.

Q. *But you realized what information you were lacking and knew where to get it.*

A. Yes, and those guys were nice to let me in. They wouldn't tell me anything now, since we've become competitive.

Q. *Your various businesses*—Ebony, Jet, *Fashion Fair Cosmetics*—*they're all black businesses. Why?*

A. They're not all "black businesses." They're all black-owned businesses. We have counters for Fashion Fair Cosmetics in over 2,000 high-line stores from Dallas to London and Paris. We're in Neiman-Marcus and Marshall Field's, in Harrods of London and Printemps and Galeries Lafayette Haussmann of Paris. We accept dollar bills, pounds, and francs from any customer.

The last frontier in America is the economic barrier—white entrepreneurs can sell to 100 percent of the market, while black entrepreneurs have been confined to 10 or 20 percent of the market.

Happily, this situation is slowly changing since blacks and Hispanics are becoming a new majority in the big American cities. Managers have a new respect for the $280 billion black-consumer market.

Q. *Have you tried to venture into a business for the white marketplace?*

A. Yes. I've had some frustrating experiences. One guy offered to sell me *Quick*, a pocket-size magazine for whites, similar to *Jet*. He gave me the name of the *Quick* editors. I went around, and not a single one would work for me.

Q. *Why not?*

A. Because I was black and they were white. Even now it's hard to get a top white person to work for me. They'll sign on as consultants, lawyers, or accountants, but most will not work full time here.

Q. *Colin Powell has white people working for him—millions of them.*

A. The military is the most integrated part of our society. It's not typical. I don't know of one black CEO of a Fortune 500 company, or even a Forbes 1,000 company. I think that racism is worse now than when I started. It's simply gone underground.

Q. *Why do you think, a century after emancipation and a generation after Martin Luther King's marches, race remains America's main problem?*

A. Because we changed the laws but couldn't change the hearts. The legacy of racism is handed down. Still, I'm optimistic about the future. Blacks will get more education and become better at their jobs. More blacks will make themselves indispensable.

Q. *With all the problems in the black community, does your feel-good approach still work with* Ebony *and* Jet?

A. Yes, circulation keeps going up. But we've never had only a feel-good approach. We said in the first issue of *Ebony* that we "will try to mirror the happier side of Negro life—the positive, everyday achievements from Harlem to Hollywood. But when we talk about race as the number-one problem in America, we'll talk turkey." We still write about the achievements of blacks and still talk turkey about race.

Q. *Don't you get criticized for happy stories when there are problems with drugs, crime, dropouts, and teenage pregnancies?*

A. We deal with those issues. In fact, we've won awards for stories and special issues on crime, drugs, and teenage pregnancies.

When I was young, my mother would give me castor oil for every illness I had or could have had. I'd run and hide under the bed, until finally she got smart and gave me castor oil in orange juice. We put an entertainer on the cover as the orange juice and have the castor oil inside the magazine. In spite of all these problems, we show that many blacks are succeeding against the odds. Our readers know there's discrimination—we don't have to tell them that—but they need to know that people can overcome it.

Q. *What were the biggest obstacles you've overcome?*

A. Finding capital during the 20 years before I could get a bank loan. I did creative financing by selling lifetime subscriptions for $100.

Q. *In your personal life, the death of your son must have been hardest.*

A. Yeah. He had sickle cell anemia, which I couldn't even talk about for 10 years.

Q. *Did you treat him special?*

A. Sure. He was special. I helped him do whatever he wanted to do. He was into racing, so I bought him several racing cars. He wanted to get married, so he got married—twice, in fact. He got his own apartment, a Mercedes, whatever.

He was a good person and handled the whole thing with great dignity. If he felt sorry for himself, he didn't let you know it.

Q. *How about you?*

A. I felt sorry for myself all the time. All the time. I lived with it for 25 years. It's something you never get over. He was a most unusual person. At his funeral, I wrote a eulogy and had somebody else read it out loud. I couldn't read it myself.

Q. *What's the main advice you give your daughter as the company's chief operating officer?*

A. To understand and inspire people. To participate in community activities. To get to know people at higher levels so that when advertising is turned down, she knows the guy at the top. I tell her, "You have to feel it. It's not in books. You need sound instincts."

Q. *What big lessons have you learned about how to get the job done in life, in business, in the black community?*

A. Keep on striving. There's no such thing as security or permanent success. To get the job done, you've got to get started. Quit talking! Quit dreaming! Quit reading! Quit thinking!

I constantly run into people who are waiting around for the right moment. There is no right moment. I was never ready to do anything I did. You make it the right time by doing it. Just begin!

THE U.S. LEADER
ELECTED BY THE ENTIRE WORLD.

Of all the business jet choices today, one line is the undisputed leader. One is chosen by more companies than any other.

Before choosing, most companies carefully evaluated several candidates. They looked at overall performance and operating cost. They compared safety records. Reliability. Cabin comfort. And support networks.

Then companies in 49 U.S. states and in 58 other nations all arrived at the same sensible conclusion. They all bought Cessna Citations.

THE SENSIBLE CITATIONS

Cessna
A Textron Company

Additional Copies

To order additional copies of *Getting the Job Done* for friends or colleagues, please write to The Chief Executive Press, Whittle Books, 333 Main St., Knoxville, Tenn. 37902. Please include the recipient's name, mailing address, and, where applicable, title, company name, and type of business.

For a single copy, please enclose a check for $13.95 payable to The Chief Executive Press. When ordering 10 or more books, enclose $11.95 for each; for orders of 50 or more, enclose $9.95 for each. If you wish to place an order by phone, call 800-284-1956.

Please allow two weeks for delivery.
Tennessee residents must add 8¼ percent sales tax.